Choose the Right A Levels

The A–Z subject guide

Ray Le Tarouilly

Choose the Right A Levels: The A–Z subject guide

This first edition published in 2017 by Trotman Education, an imprint of Crimson Publishing Limited, 19–21c Charles Street, Bath, BA1 1HX

Author: Ray Le Tarouilly

British Library Cataloguing in Publication Data

A catalogue record for this book is available from the British Library

ISBN: 978 1 911067 26 9

Typeset by IDS (DataConnection) UK Ltd
Printed and bound in Malta by Gutenberg Press

Contents

Acknowledgements

I would like to express my particular thanks to the following:

Students and staff from: Lady Hawkins School, Kington, Herefordshire, City & Islington Sixth Form College, London, Heath Lane Academy, Leicestershire, Bryanston School, Dorset, St Peter's Catholic School, Guildford, Surrey, Hereford Cathedral School, Greenhead College, Huddersfield, Accrington & Rossendale College, Lancashire, John Cleveland Sixth Form in Leicestershire, Malmesbury School Sixth Form in Wiltshire, and others not specifically named but who all contributed their insights into A level subjects so willingly. Also to the awarding bodies for their helpful advice and to the Joint Council for Qualifications for permission to use A level results for 2016 in subject descriptions. A special thanks to Della Oliver at Trotman for her help and support throughout. Last and by no means least, thank you to my wife, Patricia, for her support in my many hours of isolation in writing this book.

Introduction

This book will be of interest to students exploring A levels, and to parents/carers, teachers and careers guidance practitioners. It focuses primarily on A levels and AS levels in ***England***, where most of the recent government-driven qualification reforms have been implemented, although there is also reference to reforms in Wales and Northern Ireland. Scotland has a different set of post-16 qualifications equivalent to AS and A levels, known as 'Highers' and 'Advanced Highers', respectively.

There are two sections to the book. Firstly, **A Levels: the lowdown** provides advice on how to decide on A level subjects, key facts about A levels and factors to consider when choosing, such as recommended subject combinations. Also included is an at-a-glance guide to essential, useful and preferred A level subjects for entry to some of the more popular university courses. An explanation is provided of 'facilitating' subjects, as identified by the Russell Group of universities for entry to more competitive degree subjects, and also of 'softer' subjects that are thought in some circles to be less academically demanding.

Secondly, **The A–Z subject guide** forms the majority of the content and gives detailed descriptions of 39 A level subjects. This has all been written at a time of considerable change to AS and A levels, and while every effort has been made to ensure that the most accurate and up-to-date information is given, there may be changes where subjects are still being reformed. Therefore, this book should be read as a general guide only. It is important to look at sixth-form and college prospectuses and/or websites and to attend events such as open evenings at which you can talk to teachers/lecturers and students about particular subjects in order to get a good understanding of the courses offered.

Additional reference materials are provided in the appendices at the end, including information on alternatives to A levels, outlines of higher education qualifications and useful sources for exploring careers and higher education further.

What to think about when exploring A levels

- Why do you want to take them?
- How difficult are they likely to be?
- Do you perform well in exams?
- If your school has a sixth form, should you stay on there or go somewhere else, e.g. a college, to take A levels?
- What subjects will you need to take at A level for a particular career or university qualification you are thinking about?

These questions will be tackled, but first we must turn our attention to an explanation of the A level qualification.

Part One
A levels: the lowdown

What is the A level qualification?

The GCE (General Certificate of Education) Advanced (A) level has a long history, with the first students sitting their examinations in 1951. It was designed to be an academically demanding course of study assessed by examinations when students reach 18 years of age. The A level has been reformed in a number of ways by governments over the years, but it has prevailed. It is a qualification that, if not fully understood, has certainly been heard of by most, and it is still considered to be the 'gold standard' for entry to university and certain types of employment. When people are describing other qualifications they will often say that 'this is A level equivalent', so it is a kind of 'benchmark' against which we measure other qualifications.

Key facts about A levels

- They usually take two academic years to complete.
- Three or four separate subjects are studied.
- ***They are much more demanding than GCSEs***; rather than just repeating information, you will be required to critically analyse the work of academics and writers and express your own ideas much more.
- They are, depending on the subject, either entirely or mostly graded by exams in most cases.
- ***A levels do not prepare or train you for a job***, unlike vocational or occupational qualifications.
- To take A levels, you will need at ***least*** 5 GCSEs at grade C/new grade 4 to 5, usually to include English language and mathematics, and for some subjects you will need at ***least*** a grade B/new grade 6 at GCSE in that or a related subject. Sixth forms and colleges may vary as to whether they will require grade 4 or 5 at GCSE, so always aim for the higher grade.
- Each A level subject will be graded A* to E. A grade 'U' is unclassified, which is a fail. The grades awarded give what are called 'UCAS Tariff Points' (see below).
- They are offered at school sixth forms, sixth form colleges and some colleges of further education.
- Since September 2017, almost all A levels in England have been ***LINEAR***, which means that subjects are assessed at the end of the course. Some

subjects have a coursework/extended assignment component which contributes towards the final grade, e.g. in English literature, geography and history. In Wales and Northern Ireland, A levels have remained ***MODULAR***, which means that they are assessed in both years of study.

- Since 2015, some AS and A level subjects have been removed, e.g. health and social care, performing arts, critical thinking, applied art and design, economics and business studies, human biology, information technology. However, most can still be taken as vocational courses, e.g. BTECs (see page 180) or OCR diplomas (see page 177), which can be studied alongside A levels.
- In England the AS level is no longer part of the A level; it is a stand-alone qualification that is awarded separately and equivalent to 40% of a full A level. AS level results NO LONGER COUNT towards A level grades.
- Although the great majority of A level candidates are aged 16 to 18, A levels CAN be taken by older adults too. (I know of someone who took A level history at age 79! She got an A grade.) They can be studied part time or by distance learning, which can give flexibility around life and work commitments. See the Hotcourses website (www.hotcourses.com) for listings of subjects available.

Why study A levels?

A levels are often considered ***the*** natural progression from GCSEs, but be aware that there are other qualification pathways. See Appendix 3 on alternatives for information on these.

A common mistake is to assume that A level subjects must be relevant to particular careers. It is important to understand that A levels ***were never intended nor indeed suitable as a preparation or training for particular jobs***. A levels, ***regardless of subject***, are a good indicator of ability, and ***the skills developed from studying them are often more important than the actual subject content***. A levels develop intellectual skills and the ability to think analytically and creatively. Having A levels will enhance your employment prospects generally, as they demonstrate intellectual capacity, rather than giving you specific job-related knowledge and skills. A level history, for example, develops skills that can be usefully employed in a wide range of occupations, including those in law, business, management, accountancy, journalism, the civil service and teaching, not just by museum curators, archivists, genealogists or archaeologists! In addition, the majority of university degree courses are NOT job or vocationally specific. For example, science graduates can enter a wide range of non-science careers, including business, management and even politics! A notable example is Margaret Thatcher, the former Conservative Prime Minister (1979–90), who was a chemistry graduate.

A levels are still the standard entrance qualifications for university, but it is NOT merely a case of passing two or three subjects, e.g. at grades EEE. Grade requirements have risen significantly in recent years, especially for entry to more competitive subjects, e.g. medicine, law, veterinary and dentistry degrees, and also others such as nursing, midwifery, physiotherapy and politics, to name a few. Subject choice IS crucial where entry to ***particular*** occupations or degrees is sought, e.g. sciences will be required for many health-related subjects, mathematics will be required for a degree or higher-level apprenticeship in engineering, French will be required to study it at university. For further examples, refer to Table 3: A level subject requirements for university subjects, on pages 12–16.

Reasons for choosing A levels

By FAR the most important reasons for choosing to study for A levels are the following.

- **You have the *ability* to study subjects in much greater depth than at GCSE.** In some cases, A level subjects will be new to you, e.g. psychology or sociology, and you will need to have the right SKILLS to be successful at A level in subjects like these. For example, both of these involve essay writing, so your English language needs to be of a high standard (at LEAST GCSE grade C/4 or 5).
- **You are interested in them.** Successful students at A level are, in most cases, those who do extra study outside of lessons throughout the two years of their studies. You will need to get used to this, especially if you intend to go to university. You will have more time for private study than at GCSE, so ***learning to study independently and research information effectively are skills that you need to develop.*** Lessons will give you the basics and structure needed; the rest is down to you.
- **You need them for particular careers or university degree courses.** Examples include: chemistry and another science, most commonly biology, are required for entry to medicine; mathematics is often required to study economics; an essay-based A level is advisable for entry to a law degree; a language A level will be required in order to study language(s) and so on ...

Factors to consider when choosing A level subjects

In addition to the points above, there are other things to take into consideration.

1. **Taking certain A level subjects will open more university and career options for you.**
   This is particularly useful if you are unsure about what to study at university or the career path you want to follow. A leading group of research-based universities, called the Russell Group, produce the annual publication *Informed Choices* in which they identify 'facilitating' subjects, which are those A levels favoured for entry to more competitive universities and/or degree subjects. These subjects are:
   - biology
   - chemistry
   - English literature
   - further mathematics
   - geography
   - history
   - mathematics
   - modern and classical languages
   - physics.

The more of these that you choose, the more courses at university will be open to you. However, if you have a talent for art, design or music and think they could be avenues that you will pursue, taking the relevant A levels will enable this to happen. If you have struggled with any of the facilitating subjects at GCSE, think carefully about taking them at A level! Remember that GRADES achieved at A level are important, so you would do better to choose alternatives or even rethink your career aims. ALWAYS talk to your subject teachers and careers adviser about issues like these.

Facilitating subjects are indicated with the **F** icon at the top of the page in in the A–Z subject guide.

2. **Some university courses will have preferred A level subjects, and other subjects that they will not accept.**
   The University of Sheffield, for example, has a list of subjects that it considers develop the knowledge that is required to study certain degree subjects. The Russell Group, while advising students to take at least two subjects from the facilitating A level subjects list above, has also advised AGAINST taking ***more than one subject from the following list for entry to Russell Group universities***, and for more competitive entry subjects generally. The following have been described as being 'softer' or less academically demanding:

   - art and design
   - business studies
   - dance
   - film studies
   - health and social care*
   - home economics*
   - leisure and tourism*
   - performing arts*
   - photography
   - physical education.

   Bear in mind that some of the above subjects (marked *) will no longer be available with the change to new linear AS and A levels (although some are available as BTEC level 3 qualifications). Also, do not lose sight of your future aims, e.g. an A level in an art/design-based subject will be important if you want to train to be an architect.
3. **Get your facts right!**
   There are myths about university entrance requirements, e.g. 'You need A level law to study law at university'. ***Not true***; in fact some universities prefer students not to have taken it at A level, simply because they want them to start their degree as beginners in law. However, it WILL be accepted among the required A level grades. Universities will look at each applicant individually and consider a range of factors when deciding whether or not to offer a place, e.g. evidence that the applicant is well read, has done extra-curricular activities such as work experience that support the application, etc. ALWAYS check university websites and undergraduate prospectuses for subject and grade requirements! DON'T rely on what others say! If in doubt, check with the university admissions department or tutor.
4. **Many university courses will consider a wide range of A level subjects and be more interested in the GRADES achieved than the subjects studied at A level.**
   This is the case for the following university subjects in the great majority of cases:

- accounting
- business studies
- hospitality management
- information science
- law
- social work
- sociology
- travel and tourism.

However, there can be exceptions, e.g. if a travel and tourism course includes a language component then a modern foreign language may be required.

STEM subjects

STEM refers to subjects in science, technology, engineering and mathematics. They are worthy of attention as they are a high government and industry priority.

They are:

- biology
- chemistry
- computer science
- design and technology
- economics
- geography
- mathematics
- physics.

STEM subjects are important because they form the basis of a large number of occupations, including research scientist, doctor, engineer, accountant, software developer, pilot and architect, to name a few, as well as equipping students with transferable skills for other areas of work. However, A level results in England, Wales and Northern Ireland, published by the Joint Council for Qualifications, show that 92,163 students completed an A level in mathematics in 2016 – down from 92,711 in 2015. Also, 35,344 students completed physics A level, compared to 36,287 in 2015; and 12,477 achieved design and technology A levels, compared to 13,240 in 2015. Furthermore, there is a clear imbalance between males and females taking these subjects, with males being persistently the majority in the sciences, mathematics and computing. Sectors such as engineering have pointed out the serious shortage of home-grown engineers in the UK. Kieron Salter, managing director of consultancy KW Special Projects, said: 'The UK has a huge deficit of engineers. The sector has the potential to contribute an additional £27 billion to the economy by 2022, but only if we can fill the 250,000 engineering vacancies needed to deliver on this potential in the same timeframe.'[1]

Types of subject at AS/A level

It can help to organise subjects into groups. Some could arguably be included in more than one category, but for ease of reference they are listed as shown in Table 1 on the following pages.

[1] In Ben Sampson, 'Number of students taking A-level stem subjects falls', *Engineering News*, August 2016.

Table 1: Subject groups

Humanities and arts	• Classics, e.g. Classical civilisation • English language • English language and literature • English literature • Geography • History • Law • Philosophy • Religious studies	It is possible to select three or four subjects all from this list, but there will be a lot of essay writing! Consider taking a subject from another grouping below. This would also broaden the skillset you can offer to universities or employers.
Sciences	• Biology • Chemistry • Further mathematics • Mathematics • Physics • Statistics	Some students make all their choices from this list – but do this only if you are strong in them, as they are among the most demanding subjects. There are few instances where you would need three or even four from this list for university courses; two are perfectly acceptable in most cases, with a third and possibly fourth subject from one of the other categories to give a broader skillset. Three sciences would open all universities to you for medicine, dentistry and veterinary science/medicine, but note the above point.
Languages	• French • German • Ancient Greek • Italian • Latin • Spanish	Usually no more than two would be taken from this list. Having two languages at A level would be well respected by employers and universities, but one language is sufficient for entry to most university courses in languages. Again, consider taking one or more from the other lists to give a broader skillset.
Creative/ talent-based subjects	• Art • Dance • Drama and theatre studies • Music • Music technology • Photography	Take subjects like these only if you have a particular talent and interest in them. One subject only is advised if you want to keep university options open; e.g., include two facilitating subjects if you aspire to enter universities and/or courses for which there is more competition.
Social sciences	• Economics • Government and politics • Law • Psychology • Sociology	These are less likely to have been taken at GCSE; therefore a maximum of two from this list is advised, as these may be all be new to you.
Vocational subjects	• Accounting • Business studies • Computer science • Design and technology • Electronics • Film studies • Media studies	Avoid certain combinations, e.g. economics and business studies, or film studies and media studies, as there can be too much subject overlap. Take one or the other.

Table 1: Subject groups (*Continued*)

Subjects that are a mix of the above	• Environmental science (includes aspects of geography and sciences) • Geology (includes aspects of geography and sciences) • Physical education (includes aspects of science)	Aside from physical education, these subjects are not likely to be required at A level by universities. Avoid combining environmental science with geography, as there can be too much subject overlap.

In summary, the above factors should form the basis for choosing A level subjects; other reasons, e.g. that friends are going to a certain college or sixth form, or that you like a particular teacher, although they may be important to you, should be at best secondary to the above factors. Choosing the wrong subjects can result in frustration and affect your future life choices. ***Remember, it is YOU who are taking the subjects, not other people!***

Depending on the college or school sixth form attended, AS levels can be studied in 1 or 2 years. Examination boards have designed AS levels so that they can be taught alongside the first year of A level subjects. Some sixth forms and colleges no longer offer AS levels and concentrate on teaching A levels only. Where AS levels are not available, universities are likely to look at ***GCSE grades*** more closely as a measure of your academic potential. AS levels in England will not count towards final A level grades as they used to, but they will in Wales and Northern Ireland (see page 4).

I have heard university admissions tutors say at recent higher education conferences that where AS levels are not available, students will not be disadvantaged. However, I have also heard some say that ***the school or college must make it clear that they don't offer AS levels when writing academic references for students.***

The Extended Project Qualification (EPQ)

The EPQ is a stand-alone qualification equivalent to half an A level and is taken alongside A level subjects.

The EPQ enables students to:

- demonstrate independent research skills
- create a piece of extended writing or other piece of work, e.g. an invention, musical composition or art product
- choose a topic that they are interested in.

There are three parts to the qualification:

1. a written record showing how you managed and researched the project
2. a 5,000-word written report or 1,000 words plus a piece of work as above
3. a presentation.

- The project can be on anything, e.g. music, computing, antiques, genetics, language, literature, medicine … the list is endless.
- A supervisor supports and guides students through their projects.
- There are 30 hours of taught lessons and students are expected to spend a further 90 hours working on the project independently.
- Projects are submitted in November and May.

The EPQ is highly recommended for students applying to university, as it demonstrates the ability to write and reference academically and provides evidence of real interest in the chosen subject. It reflects the independent learning style required for university or employment.

The EPQ is worth up to 28 UCAS points where an A* grade has been achieved.

The UCAS Tariff (points system)

At this point, mention of the UCAS (Universities and Colleges Admissions Service) Tariff points system should be made. The Tariff is a way of comparing qualifications at level 3. By no means all universities and certainly not all employers use it. Some universities will express their requirements only in terms of A level grades and may stipulate certain subjects, e.g. A level chemistry at grade B.

The Tariff system has been changed several times, with a new version coming into operation from September 2017. The new Tariff originated from the Qualification Information Review 2012 and is a more accurate reflection of the weighting of qualifications than the previous system.

To get into university and certain jobs, the greater majority of points will need to have been achieved at full A level or equivalent, often in one sitting, with AS level and other qualification points being a small minority of the total required. It is a case of checking entrance requirements carefully!

Table 2: The new Tariff for AS and A levels

A level grade	New Tariff points (for university courses commencing September 2017 and beyond)	AS level grade
A*	56	
A	48	
B	40	
C	32	
D	24	
	20	A
E	16	B
	12	C
	10	D
	6	E

There is a video guide to the new UCAS Tariff on www.ucas.com, as well as a full listing of all qualifications that are included in it. GCSEs are NOT included in the points system – but do not forget that GCSE grades ARE included by universities in their decision whether or not to offer a place.

While some qualifications (such as GCSEs) are not included (at least, not yet) in the Tariff, this does NOT mean that they won't be considered. ALWAYS check with universities on the acceptability of qualifications you may have that do not appear in the Tariff.

A level links to university subjects and occupations

Below is a quick guide to the A level subject requirements or preferences for some of the more popular university subjects and those that prepare students for particular occupations. Please check with relevant professional bodies and/or universities on particular work experience and A level subject and grade requirements as they can vary.

Table 3: A level subject requirements for university subjects

University subject	Essential A levels	Useful/preferred A levels	Comments
Accountancy	None	Mathematics, economics, business. Manchester University prefers facilitating/academic subjects	A level mathematics is required for some joint courses, e.g. accountancy and economics/ finance
Architecture	Varies, but sometimes mathematics for a BSc degree, art for a BA degree	Art and design, mathematics, physics, history	Overall a 7-year training period to cover Parts 1, 2 and 3 of the RIBA (Royal Institute of British Architects) qualifications. Work experience will enhance a university application. A portfolio including drawings of your own ideas for buildings is essential
Art and design	Art	Design and technology, photography	A Diploma in Foundation Studies in art and design is recommended after A levels
Biological sciences	Biology and chemistry commonly required	Mathematics or another science	Courses are very diverse; check content
Business studies	None generally	Economics/business/mathematics	Courses vary considerably, finance-based courses may require A level mathematics
Chemistry	Chemistry plus another science or mathematics	Biology/mathematics/physics	Courses are very diverse and biology may not be required, but without it choices will be limited
Computing	Mathematics for some courses, especially computer science/ engineering	Mathematics/physics/computing	Mathematics and physics may be required for some technical courses. WIDE variety of course types

Dentistry	Chemistry and biology, some also require mathematics or physics		High grades at GCSE and A level required, work experience essential as for medicine. Expect an interview before an offer is made. UKCAT (UK Clinical Aptitude Test) or BMAT (BioMedical Admissions Test) entry tests required by some universities
Dietetics	Chemistry nearly always required, some require biology	Any sciences/psychology	Work experience preferable
Drama/performing arts	Some require English literature or language, and drama and theatre studies	Music/drama/English literature or language	Audition required for performance-based courses
Early years/Childhood studies	None	Psychology/sociology	These degrees do NOT qualify students as primary teachers
Economics	In some cases, mathematics	Mathematics/economics	
Engineering (all branches)	Mathematics, physics usually required, chemistry for chemical engineering	Subjects such as design and technology, electronics, computing, further mathematics or chemistry can be acceptable as an alternative to physics, but fewer degree courses would be open to you	Programmes such as 'A Year in Industry' can be useful. (See www.etrust.org.uk.) Check university course details for Chartered or Incorporated status conferred by degree
English	English literature or language	History/religious studies/philosophy/ modern foreign language	Alternatives include American literature or creative writing degrees
Environmental health/ science	Many courses require two from: biology/chemistry/geography/ mathematics/physics	Environmental science/geology/ economics	Some courses more science based than others
European studies	A modern foreign language	Politics/history/English literature	Can include work placement year or study at an overseas university as part of the degree
Fashion	Art/fashion/textiles	Design and technology	A Diploma in Foundation Studies in art and design (1 year) is recommended after A levels

Table 3: A level subject requirements for university subjects (*Continued*)

University subject	Essential A levels	Useful/preferred A levels	Comments
Forensics	Two sciences usually required	Mathematics	A popular choice but VERY competitive to enter. A traditional science degree followed by post-graduate forensic science qualification is the route to qualifying
Geography	Geography	Some prefer one from biology/ chemistry/mathematics/physics/ geology	Degrees that focus on human geography tend to be BA courses, physical geography BSc
History	History	Economics, English literature, philosophy, government and politics, sociology, religious studies, a modern foreign language	There is a wide variety of history degree courses, so check content carefully
Law	Generally no specific subjects, although at least two facilitating subjects recommended, including one essay based	History/English/politics or a language	Some universities require applicants to sit the LNAT (National Admissions Test for Law). Work experience can be useful. A level law neither an advantage or disadvantage
Media studies	A few courses require English language	English literature, sociology, psychology	Some courses are very practical, others theoretical, some a mix
Medicine	Chemistry, and biology most commonly required from the other natural sciences	Mathematics, physics, although a third non-science subject is acceptable at many university medical schools. It is safer to stick with a facilitating subject as the third choice	GCSE requirements are generally high (A*/8 to 9 or A/7 in most subjects), also high grades at A level. Most medical schools use entrance tests (most commonly UKCAT and in a few cases BMAT). Must have relevant work experience. Very competitive, expect an interview before an offer is made

Midwifery	Some courses require a science, most commonly biology	Biology/chemistry/physics/mathematics/psychology/sociology/religious studies	GCSE grade C/5 or above in English language, mathematics and science. Relevant work experience in a care setting useful and in some cases essential. Interview and assessment required at university
Music	For classical music courses, music plus grade 7 or 8 Associated Board qualifications		Performance-based courses will require grade 8 in a principal instrument
Nursing	Some courses require a science, most commonly biology	Biology/chemistry/physics/mathematics/psychology/sociology/religious studies	As for midwifery above
Occupational therapy	A science usually required, most commonly biology	Psychology/sociology/physical education/chemistry/physics/mathematics	Work experience in a care setting advised and a visit to an occupational therapy setting important
Pharmacy and pharmacology	Chemistry	One from biology/mathematics/physics	GCSE grade B/6 mathematics minimum. Relevant work experience useful
Physiotherapy	Biology	A second science such as chemistry, physics or mathematics is advised. Physical education	Very competitive to enter, relevant work experience and a visit to a physiotherapy setting essential
Primary education (teaching)	At least one school curriculum subject, e.g. art, biology, chemistry, design and technology, English, French, geography, German, history, IT, Italian, mathematics, music, physics, physical education, religious studies (theology), Spanish	Sociology, psychology, sport/physical education useful	GCSE grade C/5 or above in mathematics, English language (grade B/6 to teach in Wales) and science required. Work experience with groups of children essential

Table 3: A level subject requirements for university subjects (*Continued*)

University subject	Essential A levels	Useful/preferred A levels	Comments
Psychology	One from biology/chemistry/physics/mathematics required at a few universities	Psychology/sociology/biology/chemistry/physics/mathematics	GCSE mathematics grade C/4/5 or above required. Entry requirements vary, so check individual universities. Degree needs to be recognised by the British Psychological Society (BPS) and the Health and Care Professions Council (HCPC)
Radiography	One from physics/chemistry/mathematics/biology	A second science	Work experience in a care setting useful, a visit to a radiography setting important
Science-based, e.g. zoology/geology/earth sciences	Two sciences	Any other science subject or mathematics	Geography or psychology can be accepted by some universities. Check which specific sciences will be required
Sociology/criminology	None	Sociology, psychology, government and politics, law	Useful degree for entry to the police force. Graduate entry is being discussed as a future requirement for the police but not in place at time of writing
Speech and language therapy	Usually a science, especially biology. Some will require or prefer English language or a modern foreign language	A modern foreign language/psychology/English language/sociology/music/geography/history	Some universities have a list of preferred A level subjects; check with them on this. Work experience in a care setting useful, a visit to a speech therapy setting important
Sport/sport science	For sport science, one from biology/chemistry/mathematics/physics	Physical education, psychology	
Veterinary science/medicine	Chemistry and biology most commonly required sciences. A third science, e.g. mathematics or physics, would increase the number of universities that can be applied to	Facilitating subject generally preferred as third subject: English literature/geography/history/modern or classical language	GCSE requirements are high (A*/A in most subjects), also high grades at A level. Cambridge uses the entrance test BMAT. Must have relevant work experience with a RANGE of species. Very competitive, expect an interview before an offer is made

Part Two
The A–Z subject guide

On the following pages are descriptions of 39 AS and A level subjects. The same format is followed for each subject or group of subjects, the only differences being where data for individual subject examination results was not available. In all cases the source for A level results is the Joint Council for Qualifications, and those shown are for the whole of the UK in 2016. Therefore the results are for modular-format subjects, although the subject descriptions are for the new linear format. The year 2019 will be the first in which all results will be for linear-format A levels.

Facilitating subjects are indicated with the **F** icon at the top of the page.

Colleges and sixth forms may vary in their general GCSE requirements. Some may accept the new grade 4 in five subjects including English language and mathematics, but it is likely that many will expect a grade 5 in these two subjects at least, and higher if these are to be taken at AS or A level. In the subject descriptions, grade 5 has been stated as the required minimum, but be aware of potential variations – it is a case of checking entry requirements carefully!

Accounting

Accounting is about recording, summarising, analysing and communicating information about finance. All businesses, self-employed people, charities and public sector organisations have to keep this information about their money; this includes money spent on equipment, buildings, savings and investments. It also covers money owed to others, and money owed to them. The skills you learn in accounting are useful in a wide range of jobs. Accounting has a part to play in most areas of work, especially if you want to enter management or start your own business.

What do you study?

Broadly, there are two main areas covered at AS/A level.

- Financial accounting: how to maintain records of organisations' financial activities, use of ICT in accounting, double-entry book keeping and stock valuation, understanding the features of business activity, presenting conclusions accurately and appropriately.
- Management accounting: forecasting organisations' financial future, analysing and interpreting accounts, planning and decision making, appraising investments.

When you study accounting, when tackling questions you will often take the role of a mock financial adviser to a business and apply the knowledge you have learned to recommend particular lines of action to managers in order to improve business performance or deal with financial difficulties.

You will learn to:

- understand financial control and planning
- solve practical business problems
- communicate information clearly
- use IT and understand its financial applications
- make reasoned judgements
- select, organise, interpret and use information
- understand different types of business and organisation, e.g. sole traders, partnerships and limited companies.

Why study accounting?

This subject develops accuracy and self-discipline, plus ability to present information effectively. All these are skills that can be readily transferred to other subjects and occupations. Accounting students are able to interpret financial information. They also understand the importance of financial control in business success and the implications of accounting decisions. Having an A level in this subject would be an advantage for entry to apprenticeships in accounting as well as for university entry, although it is rarely, if ever, a required subject.

GCSE entry requirements

GCSE English language and mathematics at grade C/5 or above. Although not a requirement, a GCSE modern foreign language (MFL) will improve your future prospects, as the accountancy profession has identified a shortage of people with overseas language skills. Consider taking AS or A level in a MFL; GCSE grade B/6 or above will usually be required in the language to be taken at A level.

How different from GCSE?

GCSE accounting is not widely available; AS and A level build on topics introduced at GCSE, such as trial balance, accounting documentation and preparation of financial statements. Far more formulae are covered and there is greater depth of analysis of topics.

How are the AS/A level assessed?

Assessment is 100% by examination. AS level is assessed by one examination paper lasting 3 hours, split into three compulsory sections and containing multi-choice, short answer and extended response type questions. A level is assessed by two examination papers, each lasting 3 hours, in the same format as the AS level.

Combines well with

Economics/business, mathematics, law, information technology, modern foreign languages (the accountancy profession is keen to recruit people with good foreign language skills). ***It is tempting to take all business-based subjects, but there is a risk of too much subject overlap; seriously consider at least one other type of subject that develops other skills, e.g. essay writing, language or analytical skills.***

Case study

Katie, from a college in Herefordshire, took accounting A level alongside a BTEC Level 3 Diploma in Business Studies. She said:

'You really need to study hard and practise applying the knowledge you gain about accounting methods. You don't have to be brilliant at maths but you do need to have an eye for detail, be able to concentrate well and be good at spotting and avoiding errors. There isn't any algebra but there are a lot of formulas to learn and it can be quite repetitive. It is a very useful subject as the skills and knowledge you learn can be used in all sorts of business contexts. I decided to go into business administration rather than accounting but am glad that I took A level accounting as it has helped me understand the financial aspects of business and commerce.'

Higher education suitability

Not a facilitating subject, but accepted for entry to a wide range of university courses where grades achieved at A level are more important than subject content. Especially useful for business/finance-based degrees and can be used for entry to social sciences such as sociology, politics, law or psychology.

Accounting at university

A level accounting is not a general requirement for entry to an accounting degree, but will give a useful insight into the subject and relevant knowledge and skills. In some cases A level mathematics or statistics is more likely to be required for entry to accountancy.

Degree titles can vary, e.g. accounting, accountancy or accounting and finance. Content will be broadly similar, although some courses will have an international aspect and languages may also be studied and/or a period of time may be spent studying or working abroad as part of the degree. It is NOT a requirement to have an accountancy degree in order to become a professional accountant, although having one will exempt you from the greater part of the foundation stage of professional training (usually 1 year). Accountancy can be combined with a wide range of other subjects at university, including economics, business, marketing and psychology. Bear in mind that a combined degree may lead to less exemption from professional-body foundation stage qualifications because you will have covered less accountancy. Other degrees such as business, economics or management science can give some exemption from the professional accountancy foundation stage, but not as much as an accountancy degree. There are also HNC/D (Higher National Certificate or Diploma) and Foundation degree courses in subjects such as business and management, for which A level entry requirements are generally lower. These may lead to some exemption from parts of the foundation stage of training after university. Further top-up study can convert one of these qualifications to a degree by entering a degree course at year 2 or 3.

Jobs with A level accounting

There are apprenticeship opportunities at intermediate, advanced, higher and degree levels; in the latter two cases A levels or equivalent qualifications will be required for entry. The ICAEW (Institute of Chartered Accountants in England and Wales) provides a training pathway which leads to qualifications awarded by the AAT (Association of Accounting Technicians), followed by ICAEW examinations, which take four years to complete, leading to chartered accountant status. The AAT qualifications lead to the status of accounting technician, and A level accounting can give some exemption from parts of the AAT awards. ***Usually employers will require certain A level grades or UCAS Tariff points, e.g. grades CCC to ABB or 96 to 128 Tariff points.***

Aside from accounting, related occupations for people with A level accounting (and A levels generally) include working in banks, building societies, insurance and financial advice, as well as more general business administration and management.

Graduate level jobs in accounting

To work in accountancy at professional level, you would complete training and qualifications awarded by one of the professional bodies. As a general rule, any degree subject can be acceptable for entry into the profession.

- **Certified accountants** work in industry or commerce in a financial or management accounting role. They take qualifications awarded by the ACCA (Association of Chartered Certified Accountants), although ICAEW qualifications are acceptable (and vice versa).
- **Chartered accountants** usually work in private practice dealing with areas such as auditing and taxation. They are often partners (joint owners) of an accountancy practice and take a share of profits rather than a regular salary. These accountants usually qualify through the ICAEW.
- **Management accountants** specialise in financial strategy and planning and have a key role in advising senior personnel in businesses. They qualify through the CIMA (Chartered Institute of Management Accountants).
- **Public finance accountants** work in the public sector for organisations such as the civil service, local government or National Health Service. They qualify through taking CIPFA (Chartered Institute of Public Finance and Accountancy) qualifications.

Graduates complete a 3 year training contract working and studying for professional qualifications awarded by one of the organisations listed above.

There are many other occupations related to accountancy, including: quantity surveying, working in banks, building societies, insurance, pensions investments and taxation, e.g. with Her Majesty's Revenue and Customs.

Further reading

ACCA Careers: www.accacareers.com

Association of Accounting Technicians (AAT): www.aat.org.uk

Chartered Institute of Public Finance and Accountancy (CIPFA): www.cipfa.org

Financial Skills Partnership (FSP) – skills for the financial, finance and accountancy sectors: www.financialskillspartnership.org.uk

Inside Careers – specialists in finance careers: www.insidecareers.co.uk

Institute of Chartered Accountants in England and Wales (ICAEW): www.icaew.com

Art and design

Art and design concerns the communication of ideas in visual format. Students learn traditional drawing and painting skills and also new media techniques and the theoretical terms that accompany these art forms. AS and A level encourage students to explore a broad range of artists and to review their own work from the perspective of what they have studied about others. Analytical skills are also developed to help students develop and improve their own work.

What do you study?

Content depends on what is offered at the college or sixth form you attend, but courses typically can cover: fine art (using oils, watercolour and other materials), photography, film and video, including editing and directing, textiles, graphic communication, product/3D design (using materials such as clay, wood or stone to sculpture), critical and historical studies – where students study past and contemporary artists, which allows them to critically evaluate their own work. AS and A levels are largely practical courses but will include written work also, e.g. writing narratives on how work has evolved, and analysing works. Art and design by its nature is time consuming and students must be prepared to put in a lot of time in the studio at sixth form or college to perfect their work. Courses are also likely to include visits to exhibitions and galleries. ***The new AS and A level specifications have more emphasis on drawing than previously.***

Why study art and design?

The skills and knowledge learned can be used to progress into a variety of occupational areas including fine art, product (also known as 3D) design, interior design, architecture (but note other requirements), teaching, fashion/textile design, graphics, photography, film and media and art therapy. Apart from the art and design based-occupations shown below, the skills developed through study of art and design, e.g. observational and evaluative skills, are useful in areas such as advertising, marketing, public relations or working in TV and other media; all require the ability to communicate effectively in a visual format. Some university graduates move into areas such as arts administration, e.g. the running of art galleries and exhibitions. The creative industries sector is one of the fastest growing in the UK at this time, and the modern world of work is witnessing a convergence of arts and sciences, where creative skills are needed alongside the ability to solve problems and work with complex situations.

GCSE entry requirements

GCSE art and design grade C/5 or above may be required, otherwise you need to provide evidence of artistic ability through showing a portfolio of work you have produced.

How different from GCSE?

AS and A level involve a lot more experimentation with materials and techniques, and art works produced tend to be larger in scale than those produced at GCSE. Annotation of work is also important at A level and students need to think more creatively as to how they will present their work to the examiner.

How are the AS/A level assessed?

Assessment is similar across all the awarding bodies. Typically the subject is assessed by two components: a portfolio/personal investigation of art, and an externally assessed assignment in which students have an extended period of time to prepare, and between 10 to 15 hours of supervised time to produce the work required. The portfolio generally accounts for 60% and the assignment 40% of the overall AS level and A level grades (50%:50% in the case of Pearson Edexcel). Students have a choice of one or more specialisms in which to present work, from areas such as fine art, graphics, product/3D design, textiles and photography. A written narrative of between 1,000 and 3,000 words is also required to support work presented, the precise length depending on the awarding body's requirements.

Combines well with

Art and design can be combined with any AS/A level subjects; students who are considering other degree subjects or occupations should be mindful of the need to take two facilitating subjects if aiming for more competitive entry subjects and/or universities. A level English literature is useful or even required for entry to theatre design. Art and design at university requires the ability to write well, so consider an essay-based subject as one of your A levels.

Recent A level results

Total students: 43,242 **(Male: 10,315, Female: 32,927)** **Overall pass rate: 99.3%**

A*	A	B	C	D	E	U
12.2%	15.4%	29.2%	26.7%	12.3%	3.5%	0.7%

Case study

Rachael, from Lady Hawkins School sixth form in Herefordshire, took A level art and design. She said:

'I have always had a passion for painting, so this was my first choice of subject to study at A level. We studied various methods of painting by different artists and were supported to explore and discover our own style of painting. How you present work to the examiners is very important and you also need to put in a lot of time in the studio perfecting your work. I would say that if you enjoy art, you will definitely find something on this course to help you develop your skills and expand your knowledge of different skills and techniques.'

Higher education suitability

A particularly useful or even required subject for entry to creative industry degree/HND/Foundation degree courses such as photography, architecture, costume design, lighting design, graphics. For architecture, A level mathematics and/or a science (most commonly physics) is often required.

Art and design at university

For degrees, A levels are required but many universities and specialist art and design colleges require applicants to complete the Diploma in Foundation Studies in art and design *after* A level/AS levels. Students usually need at least one AS level or A level (preferably art and design) for entry to the diploma. University application is usually made during the foundation year; some art and design courses have a later deadline for applications (24 March) to allow students sufficient time to assemble their portfolio.

Degree courses at university fall into four broad areas:

- fine art
- graphics and lens-based media
- 3D design
- fashion/textiles.

Within these particular specialisms can be found, e.g. fine art blacksmithing, animation, jewellery making or interior design. Courses can be specialist or more broad in their approach. ***Be prepared to write essays! Art and design degrees will require you to explain and communicate your ideas.*** There are HNC/D (Higher National Certificate or Diploma) and Foundation degree courses in subjects such as interior design, graphic illustration, landscape design and furniture making. Entry requirements are generally lower. The Diploma in Foundation Studies may also be required or preferred.

Jobs with A level art and design

There are relatively few jobs or apprenticeships at this level which involve the use of art and design as a subject, although there can be vacancies in occupations such as studio junior in graphics or multimedia design (including website or games design), in visual merchandising (the design and making of display areas in retail), interior design, printing, in photography assistant roles or working in art materials and equipment-supply outlets.

Graduate level jobs in art and design

Designers tend to find employment more readily than artists, who often need to supplement their income through doing other work, e.g. teaching or unrelated jobs. Many graduates start their careers as freelancers, building up a client base and reputation before moving into regular employment.

- **Art teachers** work mostly in secondary schools with students aged 11 to 16 or 18/19.
- **Art therapists** help people to overcome physical and/or mental health difficulties through art.
- **Fashion designers** create fabrics for use by high street retailers and haute couture fashion houses.
- **Film, TV and theatre designers** create costumes and floor and lighting plans for stage and TV/film sets.
- **Graphic designers** often work in advertising designing logos, creating book covers and illustrations for magazines.
- **Product designers** work on a wide range of things, from perfume bottles to car body design.

Further reading

Art & Framing Today (Fine Art Trade Guild): http://www.fineart.co.uk/Art_and_Framing_Today.aspx

Creative Choices (Creative and Cultural Skills): https://ccskills.org.uk/careers

Creative Skillset – skills for the creative industries: www.creativeskillset.org

James Burnett, *Getting into Art and Design Courses* (Trotman Education)

Biology

Biology involves study of the structure and behaviour of all life forms. It covers topics such as cell structure, microbiology, anatomy, health, the environment, ecology and biodiversity. There are many areas within biology, including: human biology, zoology, biochemistry (the study of the chemistry of living organisms to solve problems, e.g. in food production, drug manufacturing or agriculture), biotechnology (the use of living things to make useful products or solve problems in medicine, agriculture or environmental management) and biomedical science. Biologists work mainly in laboratories, although they also do fieldwork, for example, to collect samples and do experiments.

What do you study?

Precise content will depend on the awarding body syllabus followed, but the topics covered will typically include the following.

- Levels of lifeforms: e.g. molecules, cells, tissues and organisms, eco systems meaning how groups of organisms relate to each other and their environment.
- Life continuity: chromosomes, genetics, reproduction, DNA, evolution, mitosis, meiosis, protein synthesis.
- Transport and exchange: how nutrients and waste matter are moved in plants and animals. This includes studying the role of key organs, e.g. the heart, blood vessels, kidneys and liver, plus respiration and excretion.
- Response and control: the sensory organs, the nervous system, hormone production, muscle action, adaptation to change and homeostasis (how an organism regulates itself internally).
- Energy: e.g. photosynthesis in plants, nutrition and metabolism, respiration.
- Current issues in biology: e.g. stem cell research, genetic modification, animal testing, climate change; issues that are often in the news.

The awarding bodies vary in the emphasis they place on social or human biology. Social biology is concerned with issues such as health and disease; environmental biology overlaps with environmental science and has an emphasis on more geographical and environmental aspects of the subject. Biology involves a mix of classroom and laboratory-based learning involving the conducting of experiments which develop essential practical skills using a wide range of equipment. Computer models are also used, and also analysis of number data, requiring good mathematical skills. The subject will require students to work together as well as study alone. You will need to enjoy solving problems, have good practical skills, imagination and creativity for experiment work, teamwork skills and the ability to explain your findings clearly, both in speech and in writing.

Why study biology?

Many biologists use their knowledge to solve problems and create useful products. For example, they find, test and develop drugs to treat disease; protect endangered animal and plant species; improve the way plants grow or their resistance to disease; and test blood samples in hospital to identify illnesses. A degree in a biology-based subject will be required in most cases, often with postgraduate and research-based qualifications. The skills developed in the study of biology are highly valued by employers, e.g. the ability to think logically, to research and to analyse data. These are also useful for careers such as finance, computing, management and law.

GCSE entry requirements

Usually GCSE grade B/6 or above in biology or core science and possibly additional science, plus GCSE mathematics grade C/5, but often grade B/6 or higher. Some places may also require GCSE English language at grade B/6 or higher.

How different from GCSE?

Much more complex, with new topics not encountered at GCSE. Past students emphasise the need to work hard and not to be complacent if you get an A or A* at GCSE. There is some mathematical content too, where data analysis is required.

How are the AS/A level assessed?

This subject is graded 100% by examination. Assessment is broadly similar across the awarding bodies, with AS level involving two examination papers, each lasting 1½ hours, with questions of short answer/multi-choice/extended response format, depending on the awarding body used. A level is assessed by three examination papers, each lasting 2 hours, with the exception of OCR which has one lasting 2¼ hours and one lasting 1½ hours. ***With all awarding bodies in England, at A level there is also a practical requirement (endorsement) which does not contribute to the final grade achieved but still needs to be passed.*** At least 12 skill areas must be covered, including microscopy, dissection, use of particular instrumentation to record quantitative measures and research skills. This is assessed by teachers but moderated by the awarding body.

Combines well with

Chemistry, geography, mathematics, physics, physical education, psychology. However, biology can be combined with almost any other subjects. Two sciences at A level give more university options for science-based degrees generally.

Recent A level results

Total students: 62,650 **(Male: 24,371, Female: 38,279)** **Overall pass rate: 97.2%**

A*	A	B	C	D	E	U
9.3%	17.8%	23.9%	21.6%	16.1%	8.5%	2.8%

Case study

Megan Fisher, from Heath Lane Academy Sixth Form in Leicestershire, is taking biology A level. She said:

> *'I am taking biology as one of my A level subjects as I aim to get into a medically based career and it will definitely help me towards this. I found biology the most interesting of the sciences when I was taking my GCSEs, but I was surprised at how much more in depth and detailed the A level is. It is a very interesting subject but you must be prepared to put in the extra work outside of lessons if you are to do well.'*

Higher education suitability

Apart from entry to science-based degrees, biology combines well with a wide range of A level subjects, and as a facilitating subject can be used for entry to non-science-based university courses including business, law and social sciences, as long as other requirements are met.

Biology at university

A level biology is a common requirement or at least a preferred subject for entry to a wide range of biology/biological science-based degrees and careers, including medicine, veterinary science, biochemistry, genetics, microbiology, anatomical sciences, dentistry, pharmaceutical science, marine biology, oceanography, nursing, paramedic science, physiotherapy, dietetics, speech and language therapy, psychology and sport science. A second science, most commonly chemistry, is usually required. Grade requirements can be high.

Degree courses in biology often involve a broad-based first year and then specialisation from a range of options for the following years. 'Biological science' degrees tend to be broader than biology degree courses. As with other university courses, check the content carefully to ensure that it includes particular areas of interest that you may have. Biology can be studied as a single subject or combined with others, with common examples including chemistry, geography, mathematics, psychology or sport. There are Foundation degrees such as applied biology and human bioscience, and other subjects that have significant biological content, e.g. DipHE (Diploma of Higher Education) courses in subjects such as operating department practice and biological sciences, and HNC/D (Higher National Certificate or Diploma) courses in applied biology, horticulture, animal care, countryside management, sport or conservation management. Entry requirements for these qualifications are generally lower than for a degree. There is often the prospect of further 'top-up' study to convert the HNC/D or Foundation degree to a full degree, with such students entering the second or third year of a degree programme.

Aside from these, there are many health-based professional degree courses that have significant biological content including nursing, physiotherapy, occupational therapy, speech and language therapy, chiropractic, paramedical science, dietetics and biomedical science.

Jobs with A level biology

These can include laboratory technician-level roles in places such as hospitals, schools, colleges, universities or commercial research organisations. Other possibilities include pharmacy technician, dental technician or dental surgery assistant. Further training and qualifications will be required, e.g. for HNC/D awards for laboratory-based roles. A level is by no means always required for entry to jobs like these but would be an obvious advantage. Biology is also a very useful subject for entry into health-based occupations, including healthcare assistant, where understanding of hygiene, health and nutrition is required. The logical and problem-solving skills, including number skills, can be useful for entry to careers such as finance and accountancy, where there are apprenticeship opportunities for people with any A level subjects.

Graduate level jobs in biology

There are numerous possibilities with a biology-based degree, and so it is easy to give examples of the different industries they can work in. Around 25% of graduates will move into research either at universities or with other organisations such as pharmaceutical companies, food production, medical or agrochemical companies. Some biologists work for the scientific civil service (government employees) or for the National Health Service in a wide range of healthcare and laboratory-based occupations; others go into zoological/veterinary work or do some form of consultancy work in areas such as pollution monitoring or conservation. The skills developed from the study of biology are readily transferred to non-science careers including business, management, finance and law, which all require people with high levels of problem solving, analytical, number and IT skills.

Further reading

Institute of Biomedical Science: www.ibms.org

Royal Society of Biology: www.rsb.org

New Scientist (a weekly magazine)

G. Hill, *Chemistry Counts* (Hodder & Stoughton)

M. White, *Essential Chemistry* (Usborne)

Business studies

'Business' gives the impression of private enterprise and profit, when in fact business-type activity can be applied to any sort of organisation, including schools, hospitals, charities, colleges, universities and clubs. All need to be run well and efficiently, and so business is a subject that has wide relevance. The study of business is concerned with the internal operation of the organisation, and also the impact of the external environment on that organisation. Internally, a business needs to be well managed, to have a strong understanding of its customers' needs, to have priced its products or services correctly and to have marketed and advertised them well. Suitable staff need to be recruited, trained and motivated to do their jobs to a high level. Also, accurate financial records must be maintained and the organisation needs to monitor its performance effectively.

What do you study?

AS and A level business studies enable students to understand the decision-making processes in organisations by focusing on their aims, the information required to achieve them and the factors which impact on businesses, e.g. competition, the state of the economy, laws, population change, environmental issues, interest rates and taxation. Precise content will depend on the awarding body syllabus used, but topics typically covered can include the following.

- What is business?
- Business opportunities
- Managers, leadership and decision making
- Decision making to improve marketing, operational, financial and resource performance
- Analysing the strategic position of a business
- Choosing strategic direction
- Human resources
- Accounting and finance
- The global environment
- Strategic methods: how to pursue strategies
- Managing strategic change

Business studies is a largely classroom-based subject, although courses can include visits to a variety of business organisations. Some students take part in initiatives such as Young Enterprise, which is outside of the AS and A level courses but can enhance university and job/apprenticeship applications.

Why study business?

Business studies equips students with the skills and knowledge to make effective business decisions which can be applied to working in any type of organisation. The subject is particularly relevant to occupational areas such as accounting, retail, office administration, banking, insurance, human resources, marketing, advertising and law, as well as to anyone who is thinking of setting up their own business one day.

GCSE entry requirements

Generally a minimum of 5 GCSEs grade C/5 or above, including English language and mathematics. Some places may require grade B/6 in mathematics. GCSE business is useful but by no means a requirement.

How different from GCSE?

AS and A level involve more in-depth analysis of topics that are introduced at GCSE, but new topics will also be encountered. Assignments will be longer and will need to demonstrate a higher level of understanding than at GCSE. Mathematical content will be greater, but not to A level mathematics standard.

How are the AS/A level assessed?

This subject is assessed 100% by examination. Assessment for AS and A level is essentially the same across the awarding bodies, with two examination papers, each lasting 1½ hours for the AS level, and three examination papers, each of 2 hours' duration for the A level. Multi-choice, short answer and essay-based questions are covered in the AS and A level examinations, and these can include a case study in one or more of the papers.

Combines well with

Business studies can combine with almost any other A level subject. Modern foreign languages (MFLs) are especially, useful as they can give an insight into other cultures and how businesses work in those countries. An MFL is likely to be required where business is combined with a language at university, e.g. French, German or Spanish. ***Avoid taking economics alongside business studies, as there can be too much subject overlap and some universities may only accept one of these subjects when considering applications.***

Recent A level results

Total students: 28,208 **(Male: 16,708, Female: 11,500)** **Overall pass rate: 97.9%**

A*	A	B	C	D	E	U
3.2%	11.2%	27.9%	30.4%	18.3%	6.9%	2.1

Case study

Kate, from Herefordshire, took A level business studies as one of her subjects. She said:

'I thought that business studies would be a good all-round subject and also that it would help me in my future career choices. I found it very interesting and varied. I also found the topics that are covered on the course helped me gain a number of important, transferable skills.
The knowledge gained helped me in jobs I did later, including business administration and estate agency work. Having an understanding of how organisations work and the environments they operate in definitely gave me a good basis to work in the commercial world.'

Higher education suitability

Not a facilitating subject, although widely acceptable for entry to a range of university courses, as long as other subject requirements are met.

Business studies at university

A level business is not generally a requirement to study the subject at university, although it is an acceptable subject to offer. University courses with a strong finance or management science emphasis are likely to require A level mathematics or possibly statistics. Some universities prefer a broad skillset from A level applicants, e.g. a humanities subject plus mathematics and a science.

There are several hundred business degree courses. Some are broad, covering several disciplines such as accounting, economics, finance, management and marketing. Others are more specialised and focus on a particular business function, e.g. human resources or marketing. There are also university courses where business is linked to a particular industry such as travel and tourism, retail or hospitality. More specialised business degrees can lead to exemptions from professional qualifications in particular business areas. Not all combined business and language university courses require a specific language at A level, as these can be taught for beginners at university, but you need to be able to demonstrate the ability to learn another language, hence the requirement for an MFL. Important business languages are:

Arabic, French, German, Japanese, Korean, Mandarin/Cantonese (Far Eastern), Polish, Portuguese, Russian and Spanish, all of which, depending on the university attended, can be studied in combination with business. Subjects such as law, psychology, political science and sociology, when combined with business, can enhance understanding of the business environment and/or of human behaviour.

There are also HNC, HND and Foundation degree courses in subjects such as business and finance, business information technology, marketing, e-marketing and more job-specific business areas such as events management, equine management, tourism or music management. There is sometimes the option to take a 'top up' year to convert the HND or Foundation degree into a full degree.

Some universities offer the option of a 'sandwich' placement where a period of time, usually one year, is spent working in industry (often paid) as part of the degree, HND or Foundation degree. Aston University in Birmingham has a well-established history of offering sandwich degrees and has reported that students often graduate with a higher degree classification, as they are able to relate their work experience to the subject matter well. Sandwich degrees should be seriously considered, as they also enhance employability after university completion.

Due to the wide variety of business courses at universities, check the CONTENT carefully, particularly as courses with the same title at different institutions can vary widely in terms of the topics they cover. Some will require a higher level of mathematics skill than others. Relevant work experience will enhance a university application.

Jobs with A level business studies

There are many apprenticeships in business-related occupations, including business administration, customer service, marketing including social media marketing, retail, warehousing, accounting, some law-based occupations, e.g. legal secretaries and legal executives, banking, building society work, local government and the civil service (government employees who work in places such as Jobcentres and Her Majesty's Revenue and Customs). Apprenticeships are available from intermediate and advanced levels, where GCSEs are required, through to higher and degree apprenticeships, where A levels or equivalent qualifications will be needed.

Graduate level jobs in business

Business graduates enter a broad range of occupations, although a business degree is by no means a general requirement for entry. Notable examples include the following.

- **Administration:** this can be within private or public sector organisations including the NHS, civil service or local government – administration is about the efficient running of organisations.
- **Advertising:** developing campaigns to promote particular goods or services.

- **Finance:** banks, building societies, insurance, investments, pensions or accountancy.
- **Human resources:** previously known as 'personnel management', which is concerned with the recruitment and development of staff.
- **Logistics:** the transport and/or storage of materials.
- **Management:** this can be in almost any sector, given that management is a core function of any organisation.
- **Marketing:** the identifying of potential markets for goods and services and how to sell these effectively.
- **Teaching or lecturing:** e.g. in schools, colleges or universities.

Each of the above will have its own professional qualifications where a business degree, HNC/D (Higher National Certificate or Diploma) or Foundation degree can give some exemption, depending on its relevance.

Business graduates have skills and knowledge that can be used in a wide variety of organisations.

Further reading

Financial Skills Partnership (FSP): www.financialskillspartnership.org.uk

Michael McGrath, *Getting into Business and Economics Courses* (Trotman Education)

Chemistry

This is a subject that impacts on almost every aspect of our lives, including the fuels we use, roads we drive on, pesticides used in farming, materials used to make household items, the medicines needed to treat illnesses, the food we eat, even the air we breathe. Chemistry is concerned with the fundamentals of matter, how the chemical behaviour of materials is caused at subatomic level and how life exists on our planet. It is critical to issues that are often in the news including environmental concerns, e.g. pollution control, recycling, new sustainable technologies, the development of medicines and food, agricultural chemicals, petrochemicals and the vast range of products that come from this. To be a chemist, you'll need to enjoy solving problems, have good practical skills, imagination and creativity for experimental work, teamwork skills and the ability to explain your findings clearly, both in speech and in writing. A degree in a chemistry-based subject will be required in most cases for professional-level jobs, and often with postgraduate and research-based qualifications.

What do you study?

The precise content depends on the awarding body syllabus, but in general the following will be covered.

- Structure and bonding – the periodic table, the structure of the atom, how atoms join to form molecules, what happens when bonds break and re-form
- Organic chemistry – carbon compounds, how life has evolved
- Inorganic chemistry – the chemistry of all other elements and how their properties relate to their place in the periodic table
- Physical chemistry – the properties of gases, liquids and solids, electrochemistry, energetics (what causes reactions to occur) and kinetics (how rapidly this happens)

Quantitative methods are used in chemistry, so a good standard of mathematical skill is required. The subject will involve theory-based class lessons and also practical investigations in a laboratory environment, and use of computer simulations of chemical processes and experiments that cannot be conducted in the school/college laboratory. There are potential hazards in working with toxic substances and combustible materials, so you need to be able to follow instructions carefully!

Why study chemistry?

Chemistry is an ideal subject for the enquiring and curious mind, and the career possibilities are numerous! The skills developed in the study of chemistry are highly valued by employers, e.g. the ability to think logically, research and analyse data.

GCSE entry requirements

GCSE chemistry or core/additional science grade C/5 MINIMUM, but in most cases grade B/6, and in most, if not all, cases grade C/5 or B/6 in GCSE mathematics.

How different from GCSE?

Much more complex, with new topics not encountered at GCSE, but it will develop knowledge of topics introduced at GCSE. Past students emphasise the need to work hard and not to be complacent if you get an A or A* at GCSE. There is a lot of mathematical content too.

How are the AS/A level assessed?

This subject is graded 100% by examination. Assessment is similar across the awarding bodies, with exams ranging in time from 1½ to 2 hours. AS level has two papers, A level has three. All questions are compulsory; there are no optional questions. In the OCR syllabus there are two strands students can follow: Chemistry A (AS/A level), or Chemistry B (AS/A level; also known as 'Salter'). The Chemistry B takes a more analytical and problem-solving approach to chemistry by focusing on topics such as medicines, fuels, the ozone layer and development of metals. Check with the sixth form/college on the strand offered if they use the OCR examination board. ***As with A level (not AS) biology and physics, there is now a practical requirement (endorsement) where students must demonstrate competence in at least 12 practical skills. This does not contribute to the final grade awarded but still needs to be passed. The practicals are assessed throughout the course, not in one activity.***

Combines well with

Biology and mathematics in particular, but chemistry can be combined with any subjects.

Recent A level results

Total students: 51,811 **(Male: 25,937, Female: 25,874)** **Overall pass rate: 97.3%**

A*	A	B	C	D	E	U
8.4%	23.5%	26.4%	18.7%	12.9%	7.4%	2.7%

Higher education suitability

A facilitating subject, acceptable for almost all science and medically oriented university courses, often a stated requirement for areas such as veterinary, medical and

Case study

Stacey, from a school sixth form, studied A levels which included chemistry and biology. She said:

> *'I got an A* grade in GCSE science and thought that I would find the A level easy. I hadn't realised how much mathematical understanding was needed for the A level, and maths is not my strongest subject, so I found chemistry A level quite hard. Rate equations and energetics involves maths which are areas I found difficult. I think that having a good teacher is really important as having clear explanations of the concepts in chemistry helps a lot. Practicals were fun, although they didn't always go to plan!'*

biological sciences. Suitable for entry to social science, business, humanities and art-based courses, as long as other suitable subjects are also offered. Can combine with most subjects, e.g. in a combined, joint or modular degree – but be aware of professional-body requirements for entry to certain occupations.

Chemistry at university

A level chemistry is required to study the subject at degree level, usually supported by a second science such as biology, physics or mathematics. Grade requirements can be high.

Chemistry is an incredibly diverse subject with numerous specialisms possible, e.g. biochemistry, pharmaceutical science, marine chemistry and chemical engineering. There are opportunities at some universities to work in industry as part of a degree on a 'sandwich' basis, which can be in the UK or abroad, and there are also strong links with universities overseas, e.g. in the USA, Japan and Europe, offering the chance to study in these countries. Chemistry can be studied as a single subject or a combined subject with other science-based subjects, e.g. toxicology or nanoscience, or with non-science subjects. Foundation degree and/or HNC/D (Higher National Certificate or Diploma) courses are also available, e.g. in applied chemistry or pharmaceutical science. A level entry requirements are generally lower for these qualifications. There is often the prospect of further 'top up' study to convert the HNC/D or Foundation degree to a full degree, with such students entering the second or third year of a degree programme.

Jobs with A level chemistry

Jobs and apprenticeships are at technician level working in laboratories in the pharmaceutical industry, schools, colleges, universities and hospitals. Other opportunities can be found in dental work, e.g. dental technician, or in healthcare. Career prospects will be improved by taking higher education qualifications such as a Foundation degree, HNC/D or degree which can be done part time.

Graduate level jobs in chemistry

The potential careers are too numerous to list; chemists work in many industries in the development of fuels, plastics, medicines, pesticides and foods, the manufacture of products and quality control, as well as writing for scientific journals and other publications, teaching in schools, colleges and universities, working on forensic analysis of crime scenes and advising government departments on issues such as food safety and pollution. The skills developed from study of chemistry are also very useful for careers in finance, computing, management and law.

Further reading

New Scientist (a weekly magazine)

P.W. Atkins, *The Elements of Physical Chemistry* (Open University Press)

G. Hill, *Chemistry Counts* (Hodder & Stoughton)

M. White, *Essential Chemistry* (Usborne)

The Royal Society of Chemistry: www.rsc.org

The Royal Society of Medicine: www.rsm.ac.uk

Classics - Ancient history/ Ancient languages (Classical Greek or Latin) F /Classical civilisation

OCR is the only awarding body for this subject area and offers a suite of qualifications known as 'classics' from which students choose: Latin, Greek, classical civilisation or ancient history.

What do you study?

Ancient history

- Greek history including 5th-century BC Athenian democracy
- From the Delian League to Athenian Empire
- Politics and society of ancient Sparta
- Roman history, covering Cicero and political life in late Republican Rome
- Augustus and the Principate
- Britain in the Roman Empire
- Culture and conflict in the Greek world of the 5th century BC, including Greece and Persia
- Greece in conflict
- Athenian culture
- The fall of the Roman Republic
- The invention of imperial Rome and the Roman Empire, AD 14 to 117

Also covered are social issues, e.g. the role of women, slavery and religion, literary and artistic topics including architecture, literature and sculpture, philosophy, education and economic aspects of the Greek and Roman civilisations.

Greek/Latin

Learning will be based on the study of written material, where analysis and appreciation of literary works will be involved. Visits to sites and museums linked to classics will likely form part of the course followed. AS and A level covers the following.

- Knowledge and understanding of the language: this involves translating passages from set texts and other works from Greek or Latin into English. There will also be comprehension exercises that are similar to those covered on modern language courses. In addition, prose composition involves translating from English into Greek or Latin.

- Literary knowledge and understanding: this involves study of how situations, characters, actions and thoughts are presented in Greek or Latin texts and how they can be interpreted in their social, cultural and historical contexts.
- Literary criticism: this covers the choice and arrangement of words to convey moods in Greek or Latin literature. Material covered includes works written by Greeks such as Homer, Plato, Xenophon and Aristophanes and Romans such as Cicero, Virgil and Ovid.

Classical civilisation

Classical civilisation involves the study of ancient Greek and Roman culture through literature, art and archaeology from around 1500 BC to AD 450. The new specification requires three key areas to have been studied: literature, visual/material culture and classical thought.

For AS level, all students will study the World of the Hero and one further component called Culture and the Arts. For the World of the Hero component, students will explore either Homer's *Iliad* or *Odyssey*. The works of Homer are the foundation of the Western literary canon, and the Greeks themselves considered them the bedrock of Greek culture. With their tales of gods and heroes, these works of literature form a grounding for exploration of the classical world. The component group Culture and the Arts contains two options for study, both of which include visual/material culture and literature. The choices are: Greek Theatre and Imperial Image.

For A level, all students will study the component the World of the Hero, and two further components, one from each of the two component groups: Culture and the Arts, and Beliefs and Ideas. For the World of the Hero component, Homer's *Iliad* or *Odyssey* is studied, and for the Roman epic, Virgil's *Aeneid*.

All classics subjects have lessons that include reading and critical discussion of texts, group debates and presentations of research made by students. Courses can include visits to museums, theatres, art galleries and archaeological sites, and reports on such visits will need to be written. Translations of ancient Greek and Roman literature and works on art and architecture will be studied. As with other essay-based subjects, additional reading is essential if higher grades are to be achieved. Teaching will largely be based on the study and analysis of written material, visual/material culture and classical ideas.

Why study classics?

These subjects develop an understanding of the influence of ancient history, language and culture on modern civilisation. There are few occupations that involve directly working in these subject areas, but the skills developed from them are usefully employed in a wide range of careers. The civil service recruits a high proportion of classics graduates, owing to the logical and clear thinking and reasoning that students need to complete such a degree. They can also be useful for areas such as medicine and law, for reasons that are explained below. Ancient languages provide a foundation for study of modern languages, e.g. what are known as the Romance languages – French, Spanish and Italian, for example – are rooted in Latin. The skills developed through studying classics are relevant to many careers. They include:

- understanding complex information
- forming an opinion on other people's ideas and views
- research
- finding information from different sources
- questioning whether information is biased or inaccurate
- writing skills
- problem solving
- ICT
- working in groups.

GCSE entry requirements

Very few people take Latin or Greek without having first studied them at GCSE or equivalent. Ancient History and Classical Civilisation do not have any particular GCSE requirements.

How different from GCSE?

Essays will need to be longer than those written in GCSE examinations. Also, a much greater depth of understanding and analysis will be required, as well as much more reading of set texts and additional reading as advised by tutors. See case study opposite for further details.

How are the AS/A level assessed?

Assessment is 100% by examination for all classics options.

Ancient history AS level is assessed by two examination papers lasting 1½ hours each and these cover a compulsory question on a period study of ancient Greece in paper one and Rome in paper two. A level is assessed by two examinations each lasting 2½ hours, with each containing a compulsory period study of Greece and Rome, respectively, and each giving a choice of one from three in-depth studies on ancient Greece in paper one and Rome in paper two.

AS level Classical Greek and Classical Latin (separate subjects) are each assessed by two examination papers lasting 1½ and 2 hours covering language and literature, respectively. A level Classical Greek and Classical Latin are each assessed by four examination papers, one each lasting 1¾ and 1¼ hours and two papers lasting 2 hours each. These cover translation, prose composition or comprehension. Prose composition also includes a small amount of translation and grammar questions.

Classical civilisation AS level is assessed by two examinations, each lasting 1½ hours, and the A level by three examination papers, one lasting 2 hours 20 minutes, the other two lasting 1¾ hours each. Candidates answer questions on particular areas covered by their courses.

Combines well with

English, modern languages, history, government and politics, sociology, religious studies, philosophy and history of art all combine well with classics. In fact classics can be combined with any subjects, including sciences, owing to the written presentation skills it develops. Ancient languages can be useful for medicine at university as there are many anatomical and pathological terms expressed in Latin. Latin is also useful for entry to a law degree, where legal terms are often expressed in that language. A levels in mathematics or chemistry are recommended if you are aiming to take a degree in archaeology, as scientific analyses will be used on most courses.

Case study

Libby, from Bryanston School in Dorset, is studying Latin as one of her A levels. She said:

> *'I chose Latin because I was considering doing classics at university and I got a decent grade at it for GCSE. I knew that I definitely wanted to do languages in some way and Latin provides a good foundation for the study of European/romance languages. There are a number of differences from GCSE:*
>
> - *the introduction of poetry (unseen)*
> - *there is more to learn (much more extensive knowledge of vocabulary and grammar needed)*
> - *the set texts are longer and throughout the A level course the types of questions posed require more in-depth, longer responses (25 marks in the second year) but these are the same sort of questions that you would have done at GCSE, where you have to comment on the content and style of a passage.*
>
> *There is a lot of memorising involved: vocabulary lists, grammar tables (you really need to know your noun endings for unseen poetry translations) and set literature translations. Once it comes to the exam, if you have memorised all those, then you stand a good chance of doing well. I have really enjoyed the poetry side of the course because the poems studied are some of the best in the world. I would say that it's more enjoyable than GCSE but also a lot harder because, as you progress, the content of the literature (set and unseen) gets more interesting, but this means that the Latin is usually more difficult. I would recommend the course, especially if you are thinking of doing anything classics, modern language or English based as it helps to increase your understanding of these things. Also, if you don't mind memorising many lists!'*

Recent A level results

All classical subjects

Total students: 6,581 **(Male: 2,714, Female: 3,867)** **Overall pass rate: 99.1%**

A*	A	B	C	D	E	U
8.6%	24.1%	30.6%	22.1%	10.3%	3.4%	0.9%

Higher education suitability

Ancient languages are among the facilitating subjects, and so they are universally accepted for entry to degree courses in any subject, as long as other requirements are met. Ancient history and classical civilisation are not facilitating subjects but are still widely accepted for university entry, as long as requirements are met in other subjects if applicable.

Classics at university

As these subjects are relatively rare (fewer than 7,000 students sat A levels in classical subjects generally across the UK in 2016), universities now teach them for complete beginners. To study archaeology at university, consider taking a science at A level; at the very least you will need a good grade (grade C/5 or above) at GCSE, as archaeology degree courses often involve scientific analysis.

Degree options are numerous which include single or combined classical languages, and likewise single or combined ancient history or classical civilisation subjects.

With classical languages, course content will build on the knowledge gained from A level, where it has been taken, and will involve study of many more writers. There are some degree courses where Latin can be studied in a historical context, e.g. from the end of the Roman Empire to the Middle Ages. Courses can also involve study of Greek and Roman history, culture, mythology, art, architecture and religion. Modern languages can also be studied with classical languages.

Ancient history degrees will typically involve developing general knowledge of ancient history and the skills required to interpret data in the first year. The following two years can cover a broad range of topics but may allow you to specialise in a particular area, e.g. Egyptian, Greek or Roman history. The degree may include visits to countries connected to your chosen specialism. Most degree courses will also allow you to learn an ancient language such as Greek, Latin or Egyptian. Ancient history can be combined with other subjects at university; modern languages, history of art, anthropology, religious studies or philosophy combine with it particularly well, as they look at political, cultural and religious aspects of human society. There are no Foundation degree or HNC/D (Higher National Certificate or Diploma) courses in classics, but there are related subjects such as heritage, history and archaeology at this level.

Jobs with A level classics subjects

Jobs directly working with classics for people with A levels are scarce and would include museum assistants, archaeological or heritage assistants, roles which can be available through apprenticeships. Horticulture is an occupational area which involves extensive use of Latin in the naming of plant species; zoos and safari parks use Latin to name animal species and law is a field which expresses maxims (principles) in Latin. As with ancient history, the skills developed by the study of ancient languages can be used in a range of contemporary occupations which require the ability to interpret and present information effectively, including the civil service, business administration, management, sales and marketing.

Graduate level jobs in classics subjects

Employment opportunities for classics graduates that involve working directly with classics include the following.

- Archaeologists (a degree in archaeology would be needed)
- Archivists
- Heritage managers
- Library and information managers
- Museum curators
- Teachers
- University lecturers/researchers

Postgraduate study and training would be required for all the above.

A degree in a classical subject would develop skills that can be transferred to many more occupational areas, including law, the civil service, journalism, librarianship, accountancy and business generally, as well as other graduate vacancies where any degree subject is acceptable for entry.

Further reading

A.R. Burn, *Persia and the Greeks* (Duckworth)

www.classics.ac.uk

Council for British Archaeology: new.archaeologyuk.org

Computer science

Advances in computer technology have been staggering, with applications being commonplace now that were unimaginable 30 years ago. Computer science develops logical and computational thinking skills, enabling students to understand how to solve problems using computers. It also develops understanding of hardware, software, networks and communications. The subject differs from ICT, which covers the applied use of software and the management and presentation of information. ***In November 2015, the Department for Education announced that AS and A level ICT will not be redeveloped, owing to lack of subject substance, therefore AS level ICT will no longer be available from September 2017, and A level from September 2018. Awarding bodies have recreated the subject content so that it will be available as computer science.***

What do you study?

Precise content depends on the awarding body syllabus followed, but courses will typically cover the following.

- Hardware: the computer itself and what are known as its peripherals, e.g. mouse, webcam, digital camera, printer and scanner.
- Software and systems: the identification of requirements, problem analysis, design and implementation of software.
- Software engineering: the design of solutions to particular problems, how programs are structured, program writing and using programming languages, e.g. Python, Pascal, Java, 'C'.
- Data management and presentation: e.g. database design, data security.
- The internet, intranet, the 'web' and their differences.
- Web design, including HTML and web page construction.
- The impact of computing on individuals, organisations and wider society, computer copyright.

The reformed linear AS and A level qualifications have seen a significant overhaul of content, with a greater emphasis on programming, algorithms and problem solving. Additional content can be added by awarding bodies; please refer to colleges or sixth forms for detailed specifications of courses they offer.

Why study computer science?

The skills learned from the study of computer science can be widely applied to many occupations, other subjects and personal use of computers. Students develop the computational thinking skills required to understand how computers can be used to solve problems, which is an asset for many types of work.

GCSE entry requirements

GCSE grade C/5 or above in English language and mathematics are likely to be required. To study computer science at university, A level mathematics will often be required, meaning that at LEAST a grade B/6 in GCSE mathematics will be needed, but in many cases a grade A/7. Computer science or ICT GCSE are not generally required to take A level computer science although these are useful and also demonstrate motivation to take the subject. Students who do not have GCSE computer science or ICT need to have an active interest in computers.

How different from GCSE?

Much greater depth of knowledge and problem-solving ability are required, and theoretical and practical aspects are far more detailed.

How are the AS/A level assessed?

AS level is 100% examination, whereas A level is 20% non-exam assessment activity and 80% examination. Assessment is very similar across the awarding bodies, with AS level comprising two examination papers ranging from 1¼ to 2 hours' duration, depending on the awarding body. The AQA AS level has an onscreen examination paper, whereas OCR has two written papers.

A level is assessed by two examination papers, each ranging from 1¼ to 2½ hours' duration, and all awarding bodies have a non-exam assessment which is a programming project which counts for 20% of the final A level grade. AQA A level has an onscreen paper whereas the other awarding bodies have written papers only.

Combines well with

Mathematics, further mathematics, physics; these subjects can be a requirement at A level if you are aiming to go into areas such as hardware/electronic engineering/robotics at university and higher/degree apprenticeships. The skills developed from taking A level computer science can be usefully employed in many subject areas where the ability to organise information logically and efficiently are needed, e.g. law, business and all science-based university subjects.

Recent A level results

Total students: 6,242 **(Male: 5,633, Female: 609)** **Overall pass rate: 95.8%**

A*	A	B	C	D	E	U
2.7%	13.7%	22.5%	23.2%	21.0%	12.7%	4.2%

Case study

Antony, from Accrington and Rossendale College, took computing as one of his A level subjects. He said:

> *'I chose this subject as computing is so influential in everyday life and I thought it would be good to improve my skills and knowledge. The A level was much more detailed than GCSE and included both theoretical and practical aspects of computing. The subject was very interesting but I found the programming very difficult as I had no previous experience and tend not to think very logically. The classes were split in two with one tutor covering theory, including both hardware and software, and the other tutor teaching programming using "Turbo Pascal". The project element of the subject involved programming and used the above language to produce your own working programme. My coursework was to produce a program for a video rental store. I would advise anybody thinking of taking the subject to meet with a tutor and go through the course content in as much detail as possible to see if it is something that fits your own skillset. I was fine with the theory side as I am good at retaining information but I was very much out of my depth with programming and found it to be a slog to get through the two years, which was reflected in my final grade. I would also look at whether you are planning on using the course in the future, as I feel it is too difficult a course if you just want to improve your basic skills and knowledge.'*

Higher education suitability

Not a facilitating subject, but acceptable for entry to almost any degree subject, as long as other requirements are met. In some instances it can be acceptable as a science subject. Two facilitating subjects are advised where entry to more competitive entry subjects or universities is sought.

Computing at university

A level mathematics is a common requirement for computer science degrees. Physics will often be required if the degree is hardware biased, e.g. electronic engineering/robotics.

There are many degree, Foundation degree and HNC/D (Higher National Certificate or Diploma) courses available at universities and colleges of higher education. These include titles such as:

- applied computing
- business information technology
- computer science
- electronic engineering
- information systems
- information technology
- multimedia technology
- software engineering.

It is important to check the CONTENT of university courses and not rely solely on a course title when choosing. Some courses, e.g. computer science, have a bias towards theoretical ideas, e.g. mathematical foundations of computing. There are engineering-focused areas including robotics, cybertronics, computer systems engineering and network engineering. Artificial intelligence courses involve the programming of computers to perform tasks associated with human intelligence, including planning, understanding language and identifying people or places.

A number of universities offer the Information Technology Management for Business (ITMB) degree that has been jointly developed with major employers. See the Tech Partnership website (www.thetechpartnership.com) for details. There are excellent opportunities these days to work and study abroad as part of university courses and this can do much to enhance employability after graduation. There are opportunities for degree apprenticeships in computing. Computing can be combined with many other subjects at university, the more common including mathematics, business, psychology or physics.

Jobs with A level computer science

The skills developed from AS or A level computer science are valuable to a wide range of employers, given the prominence of information technology (IT) in the world of work. Examples of occupational areas where jobs and apprenticeships can be found include business administration, financial services, logistics (warehousing and transport), marketing, including social media marketing, and end-user support, e.g. computer technicians in all sorts of organisations where IT-based issues and problems need to be tackled.

Graduate level jobs in computing

Depending on the job, some employers value proof of your abilities just as highly as academic qualifications. For example, if applying for a job as a web designer, having your own personal website would be an excellent demonstration of what you can do. By no means all graduate level vacancies require a degree in computing, although it would be an obvious advantage.

Many people go on to study for professional qualifications, such as those of BCS: The Chartered Institute for IT.

There are few occupations these days that do not involve the use of some form of ICT. Accountants, engineers, lawyers, librarians, doctors, nurses, teachers, secretaries, retail assistants, designers, scientists, farmers and many others use computers as tools to find, store or process information.

Jobs for specialists in computing and IT are to be found with the following.

- **Computing services and software companies:** the computing services and software business is one of the fastest-growing areas of information technology. Computer specialists are employed both in service companies and by the people who use computers and their software.
- **Consultancies:** organisations will sometimes hire a consultant to advise on particular IT-based issues where these cannot be resolved internally.
- **Education:** e.g. IT and computer teachers in schools, lecturers in colleges and universities, trainers in private and public service organisations.
- **End users:** (the organisations that buy and use computer hardware and software), e.g. the finance sector, hospitals, schools, colleges, universities, retailers, logistics operators (transport/haulage companies/airlines/shipping companies/railway operators), manufacturing industries, telecommunications companies … the list is almost endless.
- **Manufacturers of hardware:** this includes computers, laptops, tablets, smartphones, servers, printers, routers, storage devices and monitors.

In addition to computer-based occupations, graduates in this subject can enter many others, including management, business, finance and administration, as well as many occupations where any degree discipline is accepted for entry.

Further reading

BCS – The Chartered Institute for IT: www.bcs.org

The Tech Partnership – skills for the digital economy: www.thetechpartnership.com

Dance

AS and A level concern the practical and theoretical study of dance. Courses will typically involve choreography and performance, analysis and recording of work and the understanding and appreciation of dance in terms of content and context. While a high level of dance ability is not essential, there are physical demands and students with back or leg problems should think carefully about the wisdom of taking the subject.

What do you study?

Dance technique, the history of dance, analysis of professional pieces, choreography, anatomy and health and fitness are central to the subject. Students learn how to create and perform their own solo dances and also to perform from notated scores. Choreography covers the types of notation that are used to create pieces, and also the study of important choreographers and their work. Dance analysis and appreciation teaches students how to analyse and look at dance critically and to see how professional dance works. Students take part in practical dance and choreography classes but also must be prepared to cover theory and attend dance performances both locally and at a national level and to discuss them afterwards. Choreography of group dance, involving preparation and actual performance, are also covered. This requires students to participate actively and to work well with others.

Why study dance?

This is a subject that students take primarily because they have an interest in it and in many cases are considering a professional dance career. It can also provide a contrast to the more classroom-based approach of other subjects. AS/A level helps to prepare students for their applications to specialist schools of dance and performing arts where a diploma and in some cases a degree qualification is completed. Apart from the obvious career progression, study of dance at higher education level can lead to other opportunities such as dance therapy, working in sport and fitness, teaching, choreography and other career sectors where higher education qualifications are not specified.

GCSE entry requirements

GCSE English language at grade C/5 or above is usually required, owing to the written requirements of dance at AS/A level. GCSE dance grade C/5 or above may be preferred, or, if not taken, students will need to demonstrate an active interest in the subject, e.g. by having attended dance classes/training out of school. GCSE physical education, drama and music are useful but by no means general requirements.

How different from GCSE?

Written assignments will be longer and need to demonstrate a greater depth of understanding than GCSE, e.g. when analysing dance pieces and critically reflecting on your own performance. There will be greater participation in workshops covering topics such as choreography, dance analysis, anatomy and physiology and dance notation.

How are the AS/A level assessed?

This subject is assessed 50% by examination and 50% by a non-examination component (practical) both for AS and A level. AQA is the only awarding body that offers AS and A level dance. The AS level is assessed by two components: a practical involving a solo and duo/trio performances, and a written examination paper lasting 2 hours. The written paper contains one compulsory critical appreciation piece and a choice of one from four optional critical appreciation pieces. The A level is assessed by two components: a practical involving solo, quartet and group choreography performances, and a written examination lasting 2½ hours. The written paper contains a compulsory critical appreciation of a set work and a choice of one from four optional critical appreciation pieces. The written papers for AS and A level are a mix of short answer and essay format questions.

Combines well with

Music and drama combine well, but be careful not to narrow your future options if you are considering other university/career possibilities. Subjects that develop written and analytical skills are worth considering, e.g. English literature and/or history, biology or psychology.

Higher education suitability

A useful subject for entry to degree courses in areas such as arts management, theatre studies, community arts, music, sport or teaching. Not a facilitating subject, and for entry to more academic degrees it would be wise to have two other subjects such as those mentioned above.

Dance at university

An active interest in dance will need to be demonstrated through either study or participation. Expect auditions for performance-based courses before an offer is made. Essay-based A levels are sometimes required, owing to the written aspects of courses.

Dance courses at degree level vary in content and in their title, e.g. dance studies, dance or dance performance. Not all courses at university are intended for future performers and they can include topics such as history of dance, movement physiology, sociology of dance and dance analysis, all of which have an academic emphasis. At degree level, dance can be combined with other performance-based subjects such as music or drama, and also with other unrelated subjects.

It is NOT a requirement to have a degree in order to become a professional dancer. There are Foundation degree courses in subjects such as performing arts, dance, dance and theatre arts, community dance practice and theatre arts (dance). There are some HNC and HND courses in subjects such as professional stage dance or performing arts. Entry requirements for these are generally lower than for a degree. There are also some specialist dance schools that train talented young dancers. A list of full-time accredited dance schools/colleges offering training courses is available on the Council for Dance Education and Training website (www.cdet.org.uk).

Case study

Abi took A level dance as one of her subjects. She said:

'I love to dance and am interested in choreography so it was an obvious choice. You don't need to be a great dancer but you do need an active interest in dance, e.g. by taking part in areas such as ballet, contemporary, jazz, tap or modern. We had the opportunity to perform at festivals and on different stages including dance platforms and community dance activities, which really helped build confidence and performing to audiences. I got a much better understanding of the dancer as a performer and the significance of dance, as well as the process of choreography. We had options to study a particular style of dance and learned to gain an appreciation of the content and context of a set work. The experience of performing, choreographing and analysing dance was very good. We learned how to compose and perform solo as well as in a group and were encouraged to take every opportunity to see live professional dance performances. It's not all practical though, you have to be able to write about and analyse performances, so don't listen to people who say it's an easy subject.'

Jobs with A level dance

There are few jobs for people with A levels directly working in dance, but A level dance develops knowledge of anatomy and physiology and there are opportunities in related areas such as working in the health and fitness industry, e.g. as a fitness/aerobics instructor or personal trainer (training will be needed for jobs such as these, e.g. through an apprenticeship). Apprenticeships can arise at dance schools working with young children starting classes, e.g. ballet. There can be front-of-house and box office opportunities in places such as theatres and arts centres. Other skills such as team working can be readily transferred to many other types of work.

Graduate level jobs in performing arts

Apart from the obvious examples of professional dance or choreography, there are other directly relevant possibilities including dance therapy, teaching, theatre management and arts administration. Also, health, fitness and wellbeing-based careers are worth exploring, e.g. personal training, sport therapy/physiotherapy or osteopathy (dancers are prone to injuries!). Postgraduate study and training will be required for examples like these. Dance graduates will be able to move into unrelated fields, including business and marketing, where the degree subject is not specified for graduate entry.

Further reading

Council for Dance Education and Training (CDET): www.cdet.org.uk

Creative and Cultural Skills – skills for craft, cultural heritage, design, literature, music, performing arts and visual art: ccskills.org.uk

Dance UK: www.danceuk.org

Design and technology

Design concerns the planning, preparation, manufacture and use of an enormous range of products as diverse as perfume bottles, packaging and jewellery through to road vehicles, aircraft, ships, computers, tablets, printers, household appliances and furniture. For some products, the look and appearance will be of most importance; for others, suitability for use will be the prime consideration, alongside issues such as fuel efficiency, sustainability, minimising environmental impact from production and use, and affordability.

What do you study?

There are three strands; you would take ONE from:

- design and technology (design engineering)
- design and technology (fashion and textiles)
- design and technology (product design).

In all these three strands, there is now more emphasis on mathematical and scientific principles linked to the design and technology subjects. Some sixth forms and colleges will offer a choice from the above, while others may offer only one, so check with any places that you intend to apply to about the area(s) of design and technology they offer. The awarding body specifications comprise a range of skills and knowledge required to design, make, test and market and communicate ideas effectively. Lessons will typically be a mix of theory and practical work, including model making and use of computer aided design and manufacturing technology. There can be visits to trade shows and manufacturers, depending on the industries operating in your area.

Design engineering includes system design processes and methods, the use of 'blue sky' and incremental innovation and of new/emerging technologies. Students learn how to visualise and simulate using computer aided design (CAD) and computer aided engineering (CAE) software. They also develop an understanding of the characteristics and working properties of materials relevant to engineering, including smart and modern materials. Courses cover electronic principles, including sensing, control and output systems. Also covered are static and dynamic forces in structures, including the forces of tension, compression, torsion and bending, stress, strain and elasticity, rigidity and modes of failure. Students learn how to solve problems in system design, how to represent systems and components through the use of circuit diagrams, flowcharts and constructional diagrams and how to develop and use production plans.

Fashion and textiles requires students to have knowledge and understanding of the characteristics and properties of materials relevant to fashion and textiles design, development and manufacture. This includes learning about topics such as the sources and classification of the main fibre groups, fabrics and yarns, the production processes associated with mixtures and blends, pattern cutting, methods of joining fabrics, including the use of fastenings, the working properties and physical characteristics of fibres and fabrics in relation to their suitability for various products, re-use and recycling.

Product design involves the use of graphic techniques (free-hand drawing and computer aided design) and the use of a range of materials, including metals, wood, plastics, textiles, card and paper, depending on the product the student is producing. Students learn how to develop initial design solutions, develop, test and trial models/prototype products, develop an understanding of modern design and technological practices and consider the uses and effects of new technologies and modern materials. Issues such as waste disposal, health and safety and pollution and recycling are also taken into consideration.

Why study design and technology?

AS and A level courses teach students to deal effectively with realistic design and manufacturing issues and also to design and make their own products. This gives a useful insight into manufacturing industry and makes it a more practical subject that complements other A levels taken, e.g. mathematics and physics in the case of engineering or art and design in the case of fashion design.

GCSE entry requirements

GCSE grade C or 4/5 or above in English language and mathematics are usually required, and in some cases grade B/6 or above in design and technology or art and design GCSE.

How different from GCSE?

Projects will involve a broader range of technologies and materials, and students will have to tackle more complex issues and problems than those encountered at GCSE. Practical projects will need to demonstrate higher levels of skill and knowledge, and also the communication of ideas to a higher level, hence the importance of English language.

How are the AS/A level assessed?

In all cases at AS and A level, 50% of the final grade is based on an extended design and build project, 50% on examination. The English awarding bodies are very similar on assessment, with one written examination for AS level lasting between 1¾ to 2 hours, and a design and build/make project covering a 35- to 45-hour period.

The examinations are a mix of multi-choice, short answer and essay format questions. A level is assessed by two examinations, each lasting between 1½ and 2½ hours, and a design and build/make project spanning a 45-hour period. Examinations are a mix of multi-choice, short answer and extended response questions.

Combines well with

Depending on the design and technology pathway taken, the following subjects combine well with the subject: mathematics and physics if you are aiming to go into the design engineering sector and some areas of product design; business studies or economics if you are aiming for areas such as fashion buying.

Recent A level results

All design and technology subjects

Total students: 12,477 **(Male: 7,655, Female: 4,822)** **Overall pass rate: 98.0%**

A*	A	B	C	D	E	U
4.2%	12.1%	24.2%	27.0%	20.9%	9.6%	2.0%

Higher education suitability

A useful third subject for entry to particular degree courses, including engineering, product design or fashion design specifically. Students aiming to get into more competitive entry universities/subjects apart from design and technology-based degrees should aim to take at least two facilitating subjects at A level. Design technology can also be used for entry to architecture degrees, as long as the applicant can demonstrate good drawing and design skills through a portfolio of work.

Case study

Jack, from Lady Hawkins School Sixth Form in Herefordshire, is taking A level product design. He said:

> *'I chose this subject as it is practical. I have learned new skills, in particular how to make something from scratch. There are similarities with GCSE but the A level takes up a lot more time. I really enjoy design and technology so I don't mind this, but you need to manage your time well if you are to have enough time to get work done for your other subjects. Also, there is more written work than I expected, e.g. making a diary for the process of designing and making a product. I have been surprised how something can be made from materials. It is a fun subject to take.'*

Design and technology at university

Depending on the design and technology pathway, the following AS/A levels are often required to study design and technology at university: mathematics and physics for entry to engineering (design and technology can be an acceptable alternative to physics in some cases).

The Diploma in Foundation Studies (art and design) is often required for entry to fashion design courses and closely related subjects, as students need to demonstrate a portfolio of work for entry to higher education level programmes.

There are many design and technology-based degrees at universities with a variety of titles, so it is a case of checking entry requirements carefully.

Product design-based degrees include 3D design, product design, industrial product design, product design engineering, sport products design, special effects model making, architectural design technology. Fashion design degrees include fashion design, bespoke tailoring, textile design, fashion design and manufacture, jewellery design and fashion communication. Design engineering-based degrees include systems engineering, computer systems engineering, electrical/electronic engineering, mechanical engineering, auto engineering, software engineering. Degree courses can also have options in renewable energy systems.

Design and technology-based degrees can also be combined with other subjects, the more common including business studies or management. Design degrees often ***include*** business and innovation, as many professionals are self-employed.

In all three strands of design and technology, there are also Foundation degree and HNC/D (Higher National Certificate or Diploma) possibilities where entry requirements are lower but in some cases offer progression to degree level with further study.

Jobs with A level design and technology

The jobs listed here do not require A levels and can be entered through apprenticeships or college courses at ages 16 to 18. These include building craft/technician occupations such as carpentry and joinery, shop fitting and building services. Handcraft jobs include glassmaker, model maker, watch and clock repairer, metal engraver, ceramic pottery maker and locksmith. Engineering-based jobs include sheet metal worker and automobile engineering technician roles.

Graduate level jobs in design and technology

There are MANY possible occupations in the design and technology field, and by no means all require a university qualification for entry; some can be started through apprenticeships or college courses.

They can be categorised as follows.

- **Building** includes: architect, structural engineer (overlaps into engineering).
- **Design based** includes: product designer (this covers a vast range of industries), visual merchandiser (work in retail), jewellery/silver designer.
- **Engineering** includes: engineering draughtsperson, auto engineer, civil engineer (overlaps into construction also).
- **Food technology** includes: food scientist, food technician, dietician. ***Sciences such as biology and chemistry will be required for certain courses, e.g. dietetics.***

Design and technology students develop skills such as the ability to work things out effectively, and often have good imagination and creativity. These are skills that can be readily transferred to many occupational areas.

Further reading

Chartered Society of Designers (CSD): www.csd.org.uk

Creative and Cultural Skills – skills for craft, cultural heritage, design, literature, music, performing arts and visual arts: www.ccskills.org.uk

Creative Skillset – skills for the creative industries: www.creativeskillset.org

James Burnett, *Getting into Art and Design Courses* (Trotman Education)

Drama and theatre studies

This subject covers the practical theatre skills of acting and design, as well as the study of how to devise and stage a piece of theatre. Some talent for performing or design is needed, as well as skills in reading, researching and essay writing. Students are involved in the production and staging of a play, where their acting or design skills will be assessed. Students also cover analysis and comparison of contrasting texts to discover how plays are structured and investigate the contexts in which plays are performed.

What do you study?

Precise content, including the amount of actual performance, depends on the awarding body syllabus followed, but generally the following will be covered.

- Exploration of drama and theatre: this involves the study and analysis of two play texts (classical and contemporary) to develop an understanding of how plays are structured and interpreted.
- Theatre text in performance: this follows on from the above and involves live performance, which may be a monologue (solo piece chosen by the student) or duologue (involving two performers, chosen by the student), and a group piece chosen by the teacher.

Students need to be prepared to take part actively and so this is not a subject for those who do not enjoy group-based learning or performing in front of others. Students are encouraged to get involved with performing, directing, design, e.g. lighting, costume, sound and props. There are theatre visits to watch performances, and students create original drama presentations which are also performed. Imagination and creativity are important ingredients for success at AS and A level. Practitioners are studied, including writers, directors and designers. Playwrights such as Shakespeare and Aristophanes are studied, as well as more recent ones such as Ibsen, Littlewood and De Angelis, directors such as Steven Berkoff and Peter Hall and designers including Gordon Craig, Koltai and Taymor.

Why study drama and theatre studies?

Apart from the obvious careers in performing arts, the study of this subject helps students to develop important life skills which are useful to employers in a wide range of occupations. Drama develops self-confidence, the ability to work in a team, time management, the ability to communicate effectively with an audience, writing analytically to criticise texts and productions, self-discipline to learn lines and roles and independent learning skills. These can be readily transferred to many occupations, especially those requiring good planning, organisational and verbal/non-verbal communication skills.

GCSE entry requirements

Although useful, GCSE drama is not generally required but students need to have an active interest in drama/performing arts and it is useful to be involved with productions of some sort, e.g. amateur dramatics or youth theatre in or out of school/college. GCSE English language grade C/5 or above is usually a requirement, and in some cases grade B/6 or above will be required or at least preferred in English language and/or English literature.

How different from GCSE?

More in depth, with new topics not encountered at GCSE. Essays need to be longer and demonstrate a much deeper level of analysis. More participation will also be required in performance and/or design.

How are the AS/A level assessed?

All the awarding bodies allow students to contribute as a performer or writer/designer in the assessments they cover. Each includes a written examination for AS and A level, and the exam times range from 1½ to 2 hours for AS level, and from 2½ to 3 hours for A level. Exams are a mix of open book, where students can bring in notes of up to 500 words in the case of Pearson Edexcel, and/or a clean copy of a text for part of the examination. Coursework is in the form of performed pieces or design realisations and written assignments. These make up 60% of the AS and A levels. The written assignments require students to analyse and evaluate theatrical pieces and also to show how they produced their design or performance. Coursework assignments are in written format, ranging from 2,000 to 3,000 words, depending on the awarding body; in the case of Pearson Edexcel coursework can be presented as a recorded piece of work (10 to 12 minutes for AS level or 12 to 14 minutes for A level) or a mix of written and recorded material.

Combines well with

English literature is a particularly good subject combination with drama and theatre studies. Other essay-based subjects also combine well, including history, psychology, sociology and film studies.

Higher education suitability

Not a facilitating subject, but acceptable for entry to university generally, especially those higher education courses where AS/A level grades are more important than subject content. ***Students need to be mindful of the need to take two facilitating A level subjects if intending to get into more competitive entry universities, or where they want to keep other degree/career options most open to them.***

Case study

Oliver Rossetti, from St Peter's Catholic School in Guildford, Surrey, took drama as one of his A levels. He said:

'I decided to choose drama as I wanted to express my creativity as well as gain some technical knowledge in lighting, sound and set design to keep my options open. The skills that I would be learning would also help in my other A levels and reaching my career goal of working in the media industry. Drama was really creative and a good balance between expression through acting and the theoretical side of theatre. The theory helped to inform my acting abilities by offering alternative acting models and understanding of aspects such as "symbolism", which I not only found interesting to learn about but also had the opportunity to integrate into the lighting and sound design for the end-of-year shows. There were trips to London and other local theatre shows to gain a broad understanding of different genres. The course consisted of coursework on drama practitioners and developing your own set design as well as an exam in the second year on a play that you had studied in class.

'You don't have to necessarily be really confident on stage, as the technical side offers just the same amount of creativity while you begin to build up your confidence. Drama isn't just for those individuals looking to be actors – the subject offers really useful knowledge to help with technical subjects, public speaking and leadership. If you enjoy removing yourself from "reality" and creating another world, then drama is a great place to do this.'

Drama/acting at university

A level English literature or language is required by some universities and specialist schools of performing arts to study for a diploma or degree in acting/drama. A level drama and theatre studies is not a general requirement for degree level study of this subject, but it would enhance a university application. Expect to have an audition before an offer of a place on performance-based courses.

Students intending to make a career as a professional actor need to take care over their choice of course. A diploma or degree that is accredited by Drama UK will lead to the 'Equity Card', which means entitlement to join the actors' union, Equity, which is almost essential when looking for paid stage work. Drama schools will always audition applicants for places on such courses, so be prepared for disappointment and be persistent. There are a variety of drama and theatre-related degree courses; your choice will depend on the areas of study you want. Some courses will give technical training in lighting, sound, stage management, costume or set design. Others will provide options in areas such as physical theatre, playwriting or design. There are degrees where drama/theatre studies is combined with others such as English, music, modern foreign languages or media, but other subject combinations are possible. Apart from degrees, there are many Foundation degree courses available in subjects such as acting performance, make-up, special effects, circus arts, community dance, music performance, physical theatre, stage management, theatre arts and costume design, to name a few! There are also HNC/D (Higher National Certificate or Diploma) courses in performing arts, media and special effects and technical theatre.

Jobs with A level drama

A level drama and theatre studies will not guarantee you an acting career, nor for that matter will a degree. There are apprenticeships in areas such as technical theatre, e.g. lighting, and the business end of the industry, including box-office work and promotion. Some drama students go into community theatre or youth work.

Graduate level jobs in performing arts

Occupations that are directly linked to this subject area are:

- actor
- costume and wardrobe
- director
- drama education officer
- drama therapist
- set designer
- sound and/or lighting technician
- stage manager.

The skills developed in the study of drama can be used in a wide range of occupations where effective communication (verbal or non-verbal) is required. These include advertising, marketing, public relations, human resources, sales and event management.

Further reading

Creative and Cultural Skills – skills for craft, cultural heritage, design, literature, music, performing arts and visual arts: www.ccskills.org.uk

Equity: www.equity.org.uk

Federation of Drama Schools: www.dramauk.co.uk

Economics

Economics is a social science that describes the factors that determine the production, distribution and consumption of goods and services. Economics focuses on the behaviour and interactions of economic agents and how economies work. Textbooks often distinguish between microeconomics and macroeconomics. Microeconomics examines the behaviour of basic elements in the economy, including individual agents and markets, their interactions, and the outcomes of interactions. Individual agents may include households, firms, buyers and sellers. Macroeconomics analyses the entire economy (meaning aggregated production, consumption, savings, and investment) and issues affecting it, including unemployment of resources (labour, capital, and land), inflation, economic growth, and the public policies that address these issues (monetary, fiscal, and other policies).

What do you study?

Economics involves learning about markets, how they work, why they fail and about the management of a country's economy. As a student, you will be expected to develop an understanding of various economic concepts and theories, investigate current economic issues, problems and institutions, apply economic theories in a range of contexts and analyse the strengths and weaknesses of the market economy and the role of government in it.

Typical issues that are covered include the following.

- What causes inflation (price increases) and how can it be controlled?
- Why is competition between companies a good thing for consumers?
- What causes some countries to be rich and others poor?
- What causes unemployment?
- What causes changes in house prices?
- Are public services better if they are privatised?
- Is government intervention in the economy a good thing?
- Does immigration help the economy?

Apart from formal classroom teaching, discussions form part of the learning process, so you need to be prepared to take part in these and also to have a strong interest in current affairs and read quality newspapers such as the *Financial Times*, *Times*, *Independent* and *Guardian*. Economics students need good mathematics and English skills, as the subject requires the ability to interpret data, make accurate calculations, understand graphs and write well-structured essays.

Why study economics?

The study of economics will develop understanding of the world of business and it is therefore a key subject in a range of professional-body qualifications, e.g. in banking, law, accountancy and marketing.

GCSE entry requirements

GCSE English language and mathematics at grade C/5 or above usually required. A level mathematics is often required to study economics at university, so grade B/6 MINIMUM is often needed at GCSE.

How different from GCSE?

Much more in depth, with new topics not encountered before. Essays need to demonstrate a much deeper level of understanding and analysis. Mathematical content will also be more demanding.

How are the AS/A level assessed?

This subject is assessed 100% by examination. Assessment of AS and A levels is very similar across the awarding bodies in England, with AS level comprising two examination papers, each lasting 1½ hours, and the A level having three examination papers, each lasting 2 hours. Questions can be a mix of multi-choice, data response and essay formats.

Combines well with

Mathematics is strongly advised if you are intending to take economics as a degree at university. Economics also combines well with other social sciences and humanities, e.g. government and politics, history, geography, philosophy, and also languages. ***It is best to avoid taking business studies if you are intending to do A level economics. There can be content overlap and some universities may not accept both in the A level offers they make.***

Recent A level results

Total students: 29,385 **(Male: 19,895, Female: 9,490)** **Overall pass rate: 98.2%**

A*	A	B	C	D	E	U
7.2	22.9	30.3	21.7	11.4	4.7	1.8

Case study

Matt, from Lady Hawkins School Sixth Form in Herefordshire, is taking A level economics as one of his subjects. He said:

> *'I decided to take this as I had done GCSE business studies, which contained elements of economics and I was curious and interested to find out more. A level is demanding and I have been surprised at the range of things we have covered on the course. It's also important to read quality newspapers such as the Financial Times to keep up to date with current issues in economics. It is vital to check out the subjects that interest you so that you fully understand what they involve.'*

Higher education suitability

Not a facilitating subject, but widely accepted for entry to any degree subject, as long as other requirements are met.

Economics at university

A level economics is not a general requirement to study the subject at degree level, although some will prefer it; others will accept business studies as an alternative. Mathematics is usually required, and in some cases further mathematics. It is important to check with universities about their entry requirements. A level grades needed can be high for the more popular university degree courses.

Economics degrees generally have a broad introduction, with compulsory mathematics and/or statistics as part of the first year. Year 2 onwards can involve specialising in topics such as econometrics (mathematical economics), political economy, international trade and labour economics. Universities vary as to whether these are compulsory or optional topics, so check course content carefully.

Economics can be combined with many subjects at university, with the more popular including politics, geography, modern languages, mathematics, accounting or business, but there are other possibilities. Economics can also be studied as a branch of applied mathematics.

There are HNC/D (Higher National Certificate or Diploma) courses in which economics features as a topic, e.g. business studies, marketing or accounting, and there are Foundation degrees such as heritage management and community regeneration and development which include applied economics.

Jobs with A level economics

A level economics is very useful for a wide range of occupations in business, finance and commerce, including banking, insurance work, retail management, accounting and working in the civil service. However, it can be used for entry to non-business-based occupations also.

Graduate level jobs in economics

A degree in economics is not necessarily required, but an obvious advantage for entry to:

- **the finance sector:** e.g. in the City of London, as an economics analyst for large companies advising on markets and products, as well as those who work as analysts of shares, bond or currency markets, and also the Stock Exchange
- **financial or economic journalism:** e.g. newspaper or broadcast media
- **multinational companies or institutions:** e.g. the IMF (International Monetary Fund); language skills may be required
- **teaching economics in schools, colleges or universities:** postgraduate teacher training leading to QTS (Qualified Teacher Status) to teach in schools, and a higher degree (masters or doctorate) will usually be required to teach in higher education.

Aside from the above, there are many occupations in which the skills learned from the study of economics can be used, including accountancy, actuarial work, financial departments of a wide range of commercial or public sector organisations (in the latter case local government or the civil service), market research analysis, and other occupations where any degree is acceptable for entry. Postgraduate study for professional qualifications will be needed for areas such as accountancy and actuarial work.

Further reading

The Economist: www.economist.com

Institute for Fiscal Studies (IFS): www.ifs.org.uk

The Society of Business Economists (SBE): www.sbe.co.uk

Michael McGrath, *Getting into Business and Economics Courses* (Trotman Education)

Electronics

Electronics is a branch of physics and electrical engineering. It is about the controlled flow of electrons and other electrically charged particles, using devices such as semi-conductors. The main uses of electronic circuits are to control, process and distribute information and to convert and distribute electric power.

What do you study?

Courses will cover the components that are used in electronic design, including capacitors, transducers, logic gates and amplifiers, and also use of computer aided design systems in electronics. The new specification will be more mathematically rigorous and include semi-conductor physics and will also be more circuit level focused. At A level, areas such as robotics, microprocessors and electronic communication systems will be studied. There are practical projects required for both AS and A level which involve designing and building and devising electronic solutions to particular problems; this is agreed with the teacher/lecturer. Electronics requires the ability to think and reason logically and to work out solutions to problems. It is a subject that will suit those with strong mathematical ability.

Why study electronics?

Electronics impacts massively on our lives: our TVs, mobile telephones, tablets, printers, DVD/Blu-ray players, road vehicles, motorways, railways, medical technology and even defence systems are controlled and managed electronically. AS and A level electronics enable students to understand the engineering principles and their applications, and to develop knowledge and skills that can be used in a wide range of occupations, including systems engineering, communications engineering, aerospace and robotics.

GCSE entry requirements

GCSEs in mathematics and science (physics) grade B/6 or above will often be required.

How different from GCSE?

Aspects of electronics will have been encountered on GCSE physics and design and technology but there will be more emphasis on practical applications in electronics. Mathematical content is far more demanding.

How are the AS/A level assessed?

Both AS and A level will be assessed 80% by examination and 20% by a practical project. The WJEC (Welsh Joint Education Committee) Eduqas specifications will be linear. The AS level is assessed by one examination paper lasting 2½ hours, comprising short answer and extended response questions. The 20% design and realisation project comprises three tasks:

- a design and realisation task to design a digital system to solve an identified problem, need or opportunity
- a design and realisation task to test an analogue circuit against a specification
- a design and program task to create a microcontroller system programmed via a flowchart to solve an identified problem, need or opportunity.

The A level is assessed by two examination papers, each lasting 2¾ hours and each contributing 40% towards the final grade, and a 20% design and realisation project comprising two tasks:

- a design and program task to create a microcontroller system programmed in assembler language to solve an identified problem, need or opportunity
- a substantial integrated design and realisation task to create an electronic system to solve an identified problem, need or opportunity.

Other awarding bodies that used to offer AS and A level electronics are moving over to other types of qualifications, e.g. Level 3 Technician Level (power network/mechatronic/design) engineering.

Combines well with

Mathematics, physics, computer science, and design and technology are good subject combinations with electronics.

Higher education suitability

Not a facilitating subject, but generally acceptable for entry to a wide range of degree subjects, as long as other requirements are met. Particularly suitable for entry to courses at university in areas such as robotics, mechatronics, cybernetics, fire safety engineering or computer games development. A university admissions tutor for an electronic engineering department said that students with an A level in electronics tend to be 'better rounded and successful in a variety of course subject areas – especially analogue, telecommunications, and microcontrollers – compared with students without the A level'.

Case study

Alan, from a college, took A level electronics. He said:

> *'Our tutor was excellent; he was an electronics engineer and so knew LOADS of stuff, especially about electronics in the real world and practical aspects of the subject. There is a LOT of maths in this A level, with many formulas and equations to learn and understand. Electronics has made me appreciate the importance of maths and science in the world of engineering and technology. It is important that the place you go to has the right equipment so that you can complete the practicals properly, so check this out when you go to any open days at colleges or sixth forms.'*

Electronics at university

To study electronics at university A level mathematics is a requirement; in most cases physics is the required or preferred second subject, although alternatives such as design and technology, electronics or even another science such as chemistry or biology can be acceptable in some cases. As with engineering generally at university, there are some that offer a foundation year for those with non-science A levels and who decide they want to study an engineering-based degree. For eligibility for the foundation route it is often a requirement that all A levels are not among the required subjects and that one only is a required subject.

There are other subject titles that should be explored apart from just electronics or electronic/electrical engineering. These include: software engineering, communications engineering, avionics, robotics, cybernetics, mechatronics, medical physics and computer systems engineering. Electronics can be combined with other subjects, most commonly physics, computer science and also business or languages. The MEng degree (Master of Engineering) is the degree to aim for where chartered engineer status is sought. Universities offer BEng (Bachelor) and MEng degree routes, with progression from BEng to MEng possible. There are sandwich degrees available involving an extended paid placement (often lasting one year) working in the UK or abroad.

There are also Foundation degree (FdSc) courses in subjects such as electronic engineering or electronic and communications engineering, and HNC/D (Higher National Certificate or Diploma) courses in electrical and electronic engineering. Entry requirements are generally lower than for a degree.

Engineering generally is a sector where employers will sponsor students while at university, but there will very likely be a commitment to work for them after graduating.

Jobs with A level electronics

There are technician level jobs in the areas listed below in graduate level opportunities. Apprenticeships can be at advanced, higher or degree level, and for the latter two, A level electronics can be among the preferred or required subjects for entry, others being mathematics and/or physics or another technology-based subject. Higher or degree apprentices will study for qualifications such as Foundation degree or HNC/D (Higher Apprenticeships) or BEng/MEng (degree apprenticeships). Apprenticeships usually start at technician level, e.g. laboratory technician, electronic engineering technician, telecommunications technician or CAD operator. Vacancies can be found on the government's apprenticeships website (www.gov.uk/apply-apprenticeship). Outside of electronics, other areas of employment are open to those with A levels or a university qualification, where the problem solving and logical thinking skills of such students are valued by employers. Particular examples include careers in finance, including accountancy, banking, administration and management generally, but many other occupational areas are possible.

Graduate level jobs in electronics

There are very good career prospects for electronics and related subject graduates. Many will work in areas such as:

- control engineering
- manufacturing engineering
- quality assurance engineering
- research, design and development.

In these, graduates will undertake professional training and development leading to the status of chartered or incorporated engineer, depending on the level of qualification taken at university, e.g. MEng is the requirement for chartered status. An electronic/electrical engineering degree will equip graduates with high-level problem solving skills which are valuable for many occupational areas, including banking, finance and management generally.

Further reading

Engineering Council: www.engc.org.uk

The Institution of Engineering and Technology (IET): www.theiet.org

English language

AS and A level introduce students to linguistics, which means the scientific study of language, specifically language form, meaning and language in context. Alongside analytical work on written, spoken and electronic language use, courses also look at how children use language and how it is used in society. Grammatical structures and speech analysis form part of English language study at this level, as well as accents, dialect, gender and age influences on its use.

What do you study?

Precise content depends on the awarding body syllabus followed. The course will involve the study of newspapers, advertisements, poetry, novels and plays. Students also get the opportunity to write an individual coursework assignment based on topics that interest them, which is worth 20% of the A level grade. As with English literature, READING is essential for success at AS/A level, including reading beyond the set texts for the course. Regularly reading newspapers is recommended, and also active listening to conversations, including your own. This is useful for study of the spoken word, which forms part of the syllabus. Typical areas covered include the following.

- Study of language: this includes word structure, grammar, sentence construction, typography (the typeface and layout of newspapers, for example) and phonology (the sounds of words and how these are formed).
- 'Genderlect': the speech used by particular genders.
- Dialect: the type of language used in particular regions.
- How language has changed over time (English language has changed radically since the Middle Ages), and how we vary the language we use according to the social situation we are in at particular times.
- Language in the media and child language acquisition and development.
- Language representation: this includes language used by particular occupations where jargon is used, slang and taboo language and the philosophy of language.
- How speech and writing differ: this includes the study of a variety of media, including advertisements and newspapers.
- Writing for particular purposes and audiences: how to write effectively for the people you are writing for.

Why study English language?

English language develops strong skills of self-expression and also an understanding of how language works. These can be usefully applied in a wide range of careers where such skills are required. Examples include speech and language therapy, law, journalism, teaching, a wide range of business-based occupations and working in social welfare, where the ability to communicate with others effectively is essential. Our language also enables us to understand our own identity and our view of the world around us.

GCSE entry requirements

GCSE grade C/5 in English language and English literature are a MINIMUM, but many colleges/sixth forms will require at least grade B/6 in both subjects.

How different from GCSE?

AS and A level build on knowledge gained at GCSE but rely on your ability to use information sources a lot more. Essays will be longer and need to demonstrate a greater depth of understanding. Far greater analysis of written and spoken language is involved than at GCSE, with new topics also encountered.

How are the AS/A level assessed?

This subject is assessed 80% by examination and 20% by an extended written assignment. Assessment of the AS and A level qualifications is very similar across the English awarding bodies, involving two examinations of 1½ hours each at AS level, and two examinations, each of 2½ hours' duration, at A level. The Pearson Edexcel A level involves three examination papers ranging from 1 hour's to 2¼ hours' duration. All awarding bodies require students to write two assignments involving a student investigation and original piece of writing/commentary totalling anything from 2,000 to 3,500 words.

Combines well with

Can be combined with a wide range of subjects at AS/A level, but particularly good subjects to combine with it include: English literature, modern foreign and/or classical languages, government and politics, history, philosophy, psychology and sociology. English language is a useful subject to take with A level art and design (art degree students need to able to write good essays!). Students aiming to take a degree in speech and language therapy are advised to take a science subject at A level, biology being the most commonly preferred or required subject by universities.

Case study

Gemma took A level English language. She said:

> *'I chose this subject because I enjoy reading, current affairs and language learning and went on to do a language-related degree. I wanted to better understand the linguistic choices that people make when they express themselves in written and spoken form, for what audiences and for what purposes. This helped me to become better at writing and public speaking, as well as critically engaging with texts.*
>
> *'We did do some transcription at GCSE which were English language skills, so a basic understanding of the way that people speak. A level took this to another level, looking at different forms of speech, writing, audiences and purposes. We also then applied this learning to our own speaking and writing. I really enjoyed studying English language as it helped me to better understand the world around me. Also, learning elements of English grammar helped in learning foreign languages and their grammar. We read lots of interesting letters, articles, speeches, conversation transcripts and watched documentaries and news broadcasts too. Part of our exam then included us creating a letter from one character to another in a book we'd studied, at a certain point in the story, about a certain topic. We then wrote a short explanation of some of the choices we made in our writing and why. We learned to understand the way language is used, in different contexts suited to the different audiences and the speaker's/writer's purpose. This is a really useful and applicable subject to anyone keen to better understand speech and writing in the world around them, as well as to improve their own. It would particularly enable better communication and analysis, whether complementing humanities and arts subjects or adding balance to science-based interests.'*

Higher education suitability

Not a facilitating subject, but widely accepted for entry to many higher education courses, especially those where strong written communication skills are required.

English language at university

For entry to a degree in English language, A level English language is often required. ***A modern foreign or classical language is strongly advised if you are intending to study linguistics at university.***

A degree course will cover areas such as the historical, social and geographical varieties of English language and the study of linguistics, meaning the scientific study of language and its structure. There are also combined degrees such as English language and literature, or a degree in creative writing. As with other school curriculum-type subjects, a degree in English language or literature can also involve the study of education, leading to a BEd or BA (Bachelor of Arts) degree with QTS (Qualified Teacher Status). English language can be combined with many other subjects at university, most commonly history or modern languages.

Jobs with A level English language

The skills developed from studying English language at A level can be usefully employed in a wide range of jobs where effective spoken and written communication skills are required. Examples include secretarial/business administration-based occupations, including legal or medical secretarial work, teaching assistants, library assistants, office-based jobs in local government and the civil service.

Graduate level jobs in English language

Given the importance of effective communication skills, a degree in English language is useful (but by no means a requirement) for entry to a wide variety of careers where a degree is often required, including teaching, law, media-based/connected occupations, such as journalism, public relations and scriptwriting, accountancy, administration and management, advertising copywriting, marketing and publishing.

Further reading

The Chartered Institute of Journalists (CIoJ): www.cioj.co.uk

The Institute of Translation and Interpreting (ITI): www.iti.org.uk

The UK's Professional Publishers: www.ppa.co.uk

Shirley Russell, *Grammar, Structure and Style: A Practical Guide to Advanced Level English Language* (Oxford University Press)

English language and literature

This is a subject that involves the study of language and its usage in different communicative situations. Students learn to systematically analyse spoken and written language used in fiction and non-fiction material, and also how to write their own commentaries and pieces of creative work. It involves the study of a range of literary works including novels, plays and poetry.

What do you study?

Typically, a course can cover:

- investigating different types of non-fiction
- reading and analysis of literary texts, including poetry, plays, short stories and novels from various periods
- short-story writing
- the spoken word (drama and unprepared commentary)
- using different writing styles for different audiences and purposes
- writing for specified audiences and purposes.

Texts are analysed and the representation of speech is looked at alongside styles and themes.

Why study English language and literature?

The study of language and literature develops a number of skills, including summarising, creative writing, editing and commenting using a range of texts and other written materials. Students develop the ability to write fluently and coherently, which is a valuable skill in a wide range of careers requiring the ability to express oneself in the spoken and/or written word, as with English language.

GCSE entry requirements

GCSE English language and English literature at grade C/5 minimum, although grade B/6 is often required.

How different from GCSE?

See entry on English language.

How are the AS/A level assessed?

Assessment varies in terms of the number of examination papers and their duration. AS level is assessed by examinations only, whereas for A level 20% of the assessment is an extended assignment component of 2,500 to 3,250 words, depending to the awarding body used. AS levels have two examination papers, each lasting 1½ hours. Depending on the awarding body, for A level there are two to three papers, each lasting anything from 1 to 3 hours. Examinations cover non-fiction, spoken and literature-based texts requiring candidates to write analyses of the text and also their own creative pieces. The assignment typically involves comparison of a set text from a choice of pieces and one chosen by the candidate. A piece of original non-fiction writing is also required for the assignment.

Combines well with

History, modern foreign or classical languages, government and politics, sociology, psychology. AS or A level English language, English literature or English language and literature are useful if you are intending to study art and design at university, as this requires the ability to write essays of a high standard.

Higher education suitability

Not a facilitating subject, but widely accepted for university entry, as long as other requirements are met.

For other sections, refer to the separate English language and English literature entries.

Case study

Ajmal, from City and Islington Sixth Form College, London, took A level English language and literature alongside sociology and creative writing. He said:

> *'I chose A level English language and literature as I really enjoyed English at GCSE and aim to go into teaching in the future. It is very different from GCSE and involves a new way of writing and learning new things. You get to learn and understand new meanings and explanations of texts and it also allows you to see things from a new perspective. It is important to study hard from the start; you really need to do all the reading required and keep up to date with work, otherwise it can get confusing.'*

English literature

People usually read literature for enjoyment, but the study of literature goes beyond this. It enables students to see the world from different viewpoints, to experience happenings through imagination and to read in a more sophisticated way. To do well at AS/A level you will not just need to have read set texts; you will need to know them VERY WELL! A lot of reading therefore is ESSENTIAL for success in this subject.

What do you study?

Precise content depends on the awarding body syllabus followed, but typically courses will cover at least eight texts of poetry, prose and drama, including one Shakespeare play and one other text. Particular genres such as tragedy through drama may be studied, and also themes such as childhood, through study of two novels. AS/A level students explore the techniques that writers employ to create atmosphere and develop characters. Students are required to understand the context in which material has been written, and to be able interpret information effectively. Authors studied can typically include Charles Dickens, George Orwell, Carol Ann Duffy, Angela Carter and Sebastian Faulks, among others, but check this with the school sixth form or college you intend on going to.

English literature requires intellectual curiosity and a willingness to read more widely than just the set texts for the AS/A level, e.g. read other books/texts written by authors you are studying. This is especially important if you are intending to apply to universities that interview as part of the selection process, as questions will focus on reading you have done outside your A level studies. AS/A level examinations are a mix of open and closed book. Lessons will often include participating in reading aloud the texts being studied, so students need to be willing to take part in activities like this. Some texts were written to be performed, so you need to bear this in mind when reading to others.

The course may include visits to see theatre and/or film performances, but it is wise also to attend activities like this in your own time as well; this will enhance your chances of being accepted by universities, as it demonstrates an active interest in the subject. Also, get into the habit of regularly reading literary reviews in publications such as the *Times Literary Supplement* and Sunday newspapers that contain book review sections.

Why study English literature?

English literature develops vocabulary and the abilities required to write convincingly and present a case effectively. These are essential skills for a wide range of careers, especially those which require strong communication skills, including law, journalism, teaching, business and public relations, to name a few.

GCSE entry requirements

Generally grade C/5 MINIMUM in both English language and English literature, although most sixth forms or colleges will require grade B/6 at GCSE in both subjects.

How different from GCSE?

Much wider reading required than at GCSE, including works by writers beyond those required by the syllabus. AS and A level rely on your ability to use critical sources a lot more. Essays will be longer and need to demonstrate a greater depth of understanding than at GCSE. You will also probably need to make more contribution to lessons, e.g. discussions, especially where group sizes are smaller.

How are the AS/A level assessed?

This subject is assessed 80% by examination and 20% by an extended written assignment. Depending on the awarding body, AS level is assessed by two examinations, lasting between 1 and 2 hours. Likewise, A level comprises two examinations, lasting between 2½ and 3 hours. The extended essay ranges from 2,500 to 3,500 words and can be a comparison of set texts. There are optional questions at A level, e.g. World War 1 and its aftermath or modern literature (1945 to the present). Examinations across AS and A level involve open and closed book questions that are essay based.

Combines well with

History, English language, drama, art, modern foreign languages, government and politics, law, philosophy, religious studies. English literature can also can be combined with sciences as it develops vocabulary and self-expression which are important skills for scientists/technologists too. Art students at university/art college need to be able to write essays, so consider English or another essay-based subject if you are intending to take an art and design-based degree.

Recent A level results

Figures below are for English generally

Total students: 84,710 **(Male: 22,980, Female: 61,730)** **Overall pass rate: 99.6%**

A*	A	B	C	D	E	U
5.7	13.4	29.2	32.5	16.0	2.8	0.4

Case study

Oliver Rossetti, from St Peter's Catholic School in Guildford, Surrey, took English literature as one of his A levels. He said:

'I primarily chose English literature as it is a core subject and it would provide me with the opportunity to develop my writing and analytical skills, which are fundamental throughout life. I enjoyed reading literature and the ability to express your own thoughts through exploring different texts. A level gave me the chance to be more independent and explore my own texts that were of interest to me, and because the class was small the subject became more personal to me. It was a mixture of exams and coursework, however, the coursework still stands out to me now when I look back over my studies, as I could pick and choose two texts to read and then construct my own essay questions for each, to then explore. There was regular essay-writing practice, which allowed the tutor to provide constructive feedback, helping to prepare for the exam or coursework. There were opportunities to sit with the tutor one-to-one and go over my essay plan – this was a great confidence booster when this was one of the first times I had been required to take control of my own learning. There was also the occasional presentation to deliver in front of the class, which developed my public speaking skills, inevitably helping me enter university and the world of work where my current job relies on my ability to speak in front of audiences. English literature was not just about reading books, it is about you understanding meaning within context and how you develop and express your own thoughts in a constructive manner. Unlike GCSE, you have the option of exploring your own interests and your own essay questions, which gives you freedom within your studies. I would advise exploring how you learn best, whether it be through reading and writing or more practical applications, as although there are opportunities with literature to act out scenes, you are required to work more independently at home when it comes down to constructing your essay question and writing your coursework. It is also useful to acknowledge how best you revise when preparing for exams.'

Higher education suitability

A facilitating subject, and so widely respected for university entry. The analytical and writing skills gained from studying English literature are invaluable in any field. English literature is therefore a good subject as an AS or A level for students thinking of studying medicine or single sciences at university.

English literature at university

A level English literature is often required for entry to a degree in English literature and related subjects such as creative writing or American literature. Can also be used as a third A level for entry to science-based degrees of many kinds, and also for business, law and social science degrees which require an ability to research and communicate information effectively. It is often among the preferred subjects for entry to speech and language therapy degrees, where linguistic skills are essential. A science A level is also usually required for entry to this degree subject.

Degrees in English literature can vary significantly. Some will focus on more traditional writers such as Charles Dickens or William Shakespeare, but other areas of study can include women's literature, American literature, Anglo Saxon literature and language, creative writing or children's literature. English can be studied as a single subject or combined degree, most commonly with subjects such as media, journalism, history, government and politics, modern foreign or classical languages or law, but there are many other combined degree possibilities. There are no Foundation degree or HNC/HND courses in English literature, although there are applied/vocational courses such as media, performing arts, film or journalism at this level. Entry requirements are generally lower than for degrees.

Jobs with A level English literature

Examples of occupations working with or around English literature after A levels include:

- journalist (although the greater majority of journalists are university graduates)
- library assistant
- bookseller.

However, there are many more occupations which can usefully employ the skills gained from the study of English literature, including human resources, marketing, administration and management.

Graduate level jobs in English literature

There are numerous careers open to people with a degree in English literature, but the most notable include:

- journalism
- marketing/advertising
- public relations
- publishing
- teaching
- writing for a living, e.g. author.

Aside from the above, there are many other occupations where high-level communication skills are required. These include law, a wide range of business-based occupations, social/community welfare type roles, e.g. social work or youth and community work, careers guidance and professional healthcare.

Further reading

Chartered Institute of Journalists (CIoJ): www.cioj.co.uk

Institute of Translation and Interpreting (ITI): www.iti.org.uk

The UK's Professional Publishers: www.ppa.co.uk

Shirley Russell, *Grammar, Structure and Style: A Practical Guide to Advanced Level English Language* (Oxford University Press)

Environmental science

Environmental science is concerned with issues that are in the news almost daily and affect us all. These include: climate change, genetically modified organisms, nuclear power, sustainability, wind farms, acid rain, extinction of species, destruction of rain forests, organic food production, pollution, the destruction of the ozone layer, melting of the polar ice caps, the list goes on. Environmental science investigates facts about the world and the impact of human behaviour on it. The study of the earth and its life systems involves examining animal and plant life (biology), minerals and rocks (geology), the composition of the natural world (chemistry), physical forces operating on the planet (physics), and the land forms, oceans and weather and human effects on these and vice versa (geography). In addition, the human need to exploit scarce resources, e.g. fuels, involves economics, issues such as habitat destruction, impacts on particular native peoples, which involves sociology, and governmental approaches to environmental issues bring us into the realms of politics. Environmental science is therefore a multidisciplinary subject and at the heart of the future of the planet and its life forms.

What do you study?

At AS level students develop a foundation of scientific knowledge and skills associated with the environment and how it works. The four main life-support systems which are essential for life on Earth are studied: the biosphere, atmosphere, hydrosphere and lithosphere.

The A level course enables students to apply their knowledge and understand how different environmental principles are linked. Students study the use of natural resources to supply the energy, materials and food we need.

Across AS and A level courses, topics covered will include the following.

- The living environment: this includes biodiversity, study of rainforests, coral reefs and polar regions. Also covered is the relationship between living organisms and their environment, including sunlight, water, temperature, soil, climate and oxygen. The importance of conservation and how this can be achieved are also examined.
- The physical environment: the ingredients that are essential for life, e.g. water, minerals and the atmospheric gases – e.g., carbon dioxide is essential for plant life.
- Biological resources: this includes human lifestyles and their sustainability, forestry systems and food production and the environmental impacts caused by them, with possible solutions.

- Energy resources and pollution: this includes study of the reasons why certain materials cause environmental damage, e.g. fossil fuels (such as oil and coal), managing pollutant damage and looking at alternative sources of energy.

Environmental science involves a range of activities, including discussions, essay writing, laboratory experiments, e.g. measuring pollution levels in water systems, fieldwork, computer modelling, visiting sites of interest, e.g. nature reserves, zoological garden or farms, and also reading newspaper articles, watching documentaries and giving presentations.

Why study environmental science?

The issues covered by environmental science are critical to us all, and by studying it at AS or A level you will develop both a broad and in-depth understanding of important environmental issues, and will also develop skills, e.g. analysing mathematical and statistical data, that are applicable to other occupations.

GCSE entry requirements

GCSE grade C/5 or above in science, English language and mathematics are usually required. Environmental science GCSE is not usually needed as it is not always available in schools, but if it has been taken, grade C/5 or above will be required. Geography is useful but not generally essential.

How different from GCSE?

Greater breadth of topics is covered and depth of analysis is greater. Science and mathematical understanding at higher levels are required, plus practical and creative skills in planning and undertaking fieldwork. Like geography, AS/A level have a more holistic approach than at GCSE.

How are the AS/A level assessed?

This subject is assessed 100% by examination. Under the new specifications the AS level will be assessed by one examination paper, lasting 3 hours, which comprises multi-choice, short answer and extended response questions. The A level will be assessed by two examination papers, each lasting 3 hours and again there is a mix of question types as in the AS level. Each A level exam paper contributes 50% towards the final marks and grade.

Combines well with

Biology, chemistry, economics, government and politics, sociology, geography. Geography can be viewed by some universities as too similar to environmental science and they may accept only one of the subjects in the A level offers they make. This can also be the case with biology, so check with universities on their requirements and preferences. Some environmental science degrees at university can involve data analysis, and so AS/A level mathematics or statistics would be useful for these.

Higher education suitability

Not a facilitating subject, but widely acceptable for entry to university generally, as long as other requirements are met. As environmental science includes aspects of economics, sociology and politics, it can be relevant to degree courses in these subject areas, but check entry requirements carefully, e.g. economics at university will often require A level mathematics.

Environmental science at university

One or more A levels from biology, chemistry and geography are among the most common requirements for entry to a degree in an environmentally based subject at university.

There is an almost bewildering range of degrees with an environmental focus, including: environmental geography, disaster management, environmental geochemistry, environmental conservation, marine environmental science, global development and sustainability, environmental engineering (A levels in mathematics and physics will usually be required) and environmental planning. It is important to check the content of degrees carefully, as they can vary in both subject coverage and entry requirements. Environmental science can be combined with other subjects, e.g. civil engineering in the case of environmental engineering, which is concerned with issues such as waste management, pollution and land reclamation. Other common combinations are with planning, geographical information systems and business.

Jobs with A level environmental science

Non-graduate-level jobs in environmental science are relatively scarce and many people often become involved with environmental pressure groups and other organisations as volunteers. Knowledge gained from A level could be useful in preparation of publicity and the running of local-level activities. Administrative roles can become available providing office support. From A levels or even GCSEs it is also possible to get into some environmentally based or connected jobs, e.g. with water utility companies, in forestry or horticulture through apprenticeships, some of which can lead to higher education qualifications such as Foundation degrees or HNC/Ds (Higher National Certificate or Diploma).

As with other A level subjects, the skills learned from the study of this subject can be usefully employed in a wide range of non-environmental jobs, including business administration and finance, where problem-solving and logical thinking skills are required.

Graduate level jobs in environmental science

Examples of occupations working directly in the environmental sector include:

- civil servants, e.g. science officer for the Environment Agency (government)
- countryside managers
- environmental conservation officers
- environmental health practitioners
- foresters
- horticultural managers
- hydrographic surveyors
- recycling officers
- waste managers.

Aside from environmentally based occupations, the skills developed from studying environmental science at A level or higher education can be usefully employed in other areas of work. Skills such as data recording, computing, observation, report writing and effective presentation are very relevant to careers in business, for example, especially areas such as marketing, advertising and finance, but many other opportunities are possible, e.g. teaching, journalism and other occupations where employers do not specify degree subjects.

Further reading

Environment Jobs: www.environmentpost.co.uk

Lantra – skills for land-based and environmental industries: www.lantra.co.uk

Society for the Environment (SocEnv): www.socenv.org.uk

Film studies

Film is one of the major art forms of the 20th and 21st centuries, with new modes of expression and exhibition appearing in recent years. AS and A level build on the 'cineliteracy' that students will have developed since childhood, and aim to further develop their knowledge and appreciation of film. Courses will study the way that film as an audio-visual form of creative expression constructs meaning and provokes a variety of viewer responses as well as raising issues of social, cultural, political and ethical significance.

What do you study?

Precise content depends on the awarding body syllabus followed, but typically, content will include the following.

- The study of cinema topics or film movements, e.g. 1960s British cinema, Italian neo-realism.
- The study of British and American film, including how the industry works in these countries, genres such as horror and comedy, how films are influenced by the cultural period they were made in, e.g. the 1960s and 1980s.
- The study of individual films, e.g. crime culture films such as *Get Carter*, comparing films in a particular genre, e.g. remakes such as *King Kong* (1933, 1976 and 2005) or those dealing with a particular theme, e.g. Westerns such as *My Darling Clementine* and *Unforgiven*.
- Research into the work of particular film makers.
- Investigation into the meanings, messages and values conveyed through film.
- Practical exercises in film journalism, e.g. writing a critique.
- Study of world cinema, e.g. Bollywood, Japanese or Mexican cinema, 1920s German or Soviet Union cinema.
- Writing a screenplay or making a short film.

Students are expected to develop a good knowledge of a range of films, and a considerable amount of reading is also required. Good research and writing skills are essential for success in this subject. Courses can often include visits to cinemas and also residential trips to events such as the Edinburgh Film Festival. Courses will typically involve watching films and film sequences, followed by essays and case studies. Facilities available for practical work vary but can include Apple Mac media and music recording suites. Check this with the institutions you are considering attending for A levels, and also any visits such as those outlined above. ***The material content of films can be challenging, so check this carefully also. However, awarding bodies specify use of material with a classification of age 15 or younger.***

Why study film studies?

Film studies develops research and production skills which can be usefully employed in a variety of university courses. The subject also enhances students' skills of observation, critical analysis and self-reflection, plus their creativity and practical skills in audio-visual and written forms.

GCSE entry requirements

GCSE English language at grade C/5 or above will be required; some colleges or sixth forms may require grade B/6 or higher. GCSE film or media is useful but not essential.

How different from GCSE?

Much greater analysis needs to be demonstrated at AS and A level, with longer essays than at GCSE. A broader range of film genres will be encountered and analysed than anything encountered at GCSE.

How are the AS/A level assessed?

This subject is assessed 70% by examination and 30% by a practical film making project, both at AS and A level. In England, AS level film studies is assessed by one examination paper lasting 2 hours and the film making project. The A level is assessed by two examination papers, each lasting 2 hours, and the production of a 5-minute short film or a 10-minute screenplay for a short film (incorporating a digitally photographed storyboard) and an analysis of the production in relation to professionally produced set short films. WJEC (the Welsh Joint Education Committee) Eduqas will be offering linear AS and A level. The AS level is assessed by two examination papers, each lasting 1½ hours, and a film making project. The A level is assessed by two examination papers, each lasting 3 hours, and a film making project and written analysis.

Combines well with

A level art and design or photography will help to develop skills such as visual imaging and communicating ideas, which are useful for entry to university courses in film production. Such courses will likely require a portfolio of work, and film studies in combination with art or photography can help to build this. English literature develops written skills and also understanding of material that is used in film. Modern foreign languages include the study of society and culture, which can enhance understanding of material encountered in film studies. Media studies and history also combine well with film studies. ***If you want to keep other subject areas at university open also, consider including two facilitating subjects at A level if you aspire to get into more competitive entry subjects or universities.***

Recent A level results

Total students: 28,140 **(Male: 12,399, Female: 15,741)** **Overall pass rate: 99.5%**

A*	A	B	C	D	E	U
1.2	9.4	32.0	37.8	16.1	3.0	0.5

Higher education suitability

Not a facilitating subject, but generally acceptable for university entry, as long as other subject requirements are met. A useful A level for entry to degrees in English, communication studies, sociology, philosophy or American studies, as well as performing arts or drama courses.

Case study

Sennen Cork, from Malmesbury School Sixth Form, took film studies as one of her A levels. She said:

'I enjoy films and talking about them. The A level has taught me to think about film in a different way. You have to dedicate a lot of time to the subject but if you're passionate about film it feels more like fun than work. I think that a lot of people think of this subject as a kind of film club where you can mess about and watch films like Fight Club for a few hours a week. It is not true; you should only take this A level if you are genuinely passionate about film. There is a lot of terminology to learn and it is not just about watching mainstream Hollywood films either.'

Film studies at university

A level film studies is not required for degrees or other higher education qualifications in this subject area, although having studied it will demonstrate an interest and can enhance a university application.

Content can vary significantly; some degrees will focus on the critical and historical study of film, others on practical and technical skills used in film making, and others involve a combination of these. Degree courses can include optional topics such as theoretical and analytical studies, camera techniques, technical production and scriptwriting. Course titles include: film and video studies, film production, digital film and visual effects production, computer visualisation and animation, special and visual effects for TV and film. Film studies can be combined with many other subjects at university, including English, modern foreign languages or business. There are also Foundation degrees in subjects such as creative film and moving image production, film and photography, film and TV production technology, hair design and make-up for theatre, TV and film and post-production technology. There are also HNC/D (Higher National Certificate or Diploma) courses in subjects such as applied multimedia and digital film production. For these practical courses a portfolio is likely to be required, although A level entry requirements will generally be lower than for a degree.

Jobs with A level film studies

Some people begin their careers in film or television as 'runners' offering general assistance in the production of films or programmes. The website Creative Skillset (www.creativeskillset.org) advertises apprenticeships and has also established a network of screen academies recognised as centres of excellence for film education in the UK. Courses at these academies are offered at some colleges and universities and also include short technical courses. Some people start work in the industry in advertising and distribution of films into cinema, or in marketing or administration roles.

Graduate level jobs in film studies

Even with a degree, you need to be prepared to start working at a junior level in order to take further training as required. Making contacts with people in the industry is essential for success; it is often more a case of 'who you know rather than what you know' that can lead to opportunities. The sorts of jobs that can be open include:

- assistant directors – there are different levels of these
- camera operators
- designers, e.g. set/costume
- production assistants (or 'runners')
- scriptwriters, e.g. for radio/TV/film

Further examples of occupations can be found on the Creative Skillset website. Aside from the above, the skills developed from studying film can be usefully employed in occupations in marketing, journalism, arts administration, publishing and a wide range of other roles including retail, finance or management generally.

Further reading

British Film Institute: www.bfi.org.uk/education

Creative Skillset: www.creativeskillset.org/careers

National Film and Television School: www.nfts.co.uk

Geography

Geography involves the study of global systems and physical processes in the world and the impact of humans on the earth. It is a subject that would be of interest to those who want to learn more about a range of current issues, many of which are regularly in the news, including globalisation, population growth, food shortages, immigration, agriculture and environmental issues including climate change and sustainability.

What do you study?

The precise content depends on the awarding body syllabus followed, but the study of geography is divided into two branches.

- Human geography: this looks at human activities in their physical settings, covering topics such as food shortages, conflict, immigration, population change and sustainability.
- Physical geography: this focuses on the earth and its physical structure and processes that occur on and above its surface. Climate is included in this, and also hazards such as tsunamis, earthquakes and volcanic eruptions.

Human geography focuses on the following.

- Economic geography: the distribution of resources, including food production, agriculture, health, industrial development, energy and transportation.
- Management of human geographical processes through the use of planning systems.
- Population: global population change, migration and resources.
- Settlement: the location and character of human settlements such as cities, towns and villages, why and how they grow or decline.

Physical geography includes the following.

- Biogeography: this covers ecosystems, which are communities of organisms and their environment, vegetation and soils.
- Coastal studies: the processes that form coastlines and the impact of human activity on them.
- Geomorphology: the forming of the Earth's surface through denudation (weathering and erosion), plate tectonics which cause phenomena such as mountains and earthquakes, the formation of glaciers and deserts.
- Hydrology: the study of water on and above the earth's surface, evaporation, rainfall, the rivers and oceans and applied hydrology – the management of water through dams, irrigation, hydroelectric power and flood prevention.
- The atmosphere: climate, weather, pollution, global warming and its causes, the impacts of these phenomena on humanity.

Learning will involve formal classroom teaching, and also group discussions. There is a fieldwork project/study for the A level which accounts for 20% of the overall grade. This involves collecting and measuring data, conducting surveys, using questionnaires and interviewing people. Fieldwork may be in the local area or further away, covering a variety of geographical settings. Students learn how to obtain, record, classify and interpret data from a number of sources, including the use of software to handle geographical data.

Why study geography?

Geographers are highly employable, generally owing to the transferable skills they learn, which are described below.

GCSE entry requirements

GCSEs grade B/6 or above are often required in English language and mathematics, owing to the numerical/statistical and written demands of AS/A level. GCSE geography is not always required, although some knowledge of the topics covered will be expected.

How different from GCSE?

A natural progression from GCSE, but much more in depth. A level takes a broader and more holistic approach to the study of geography. Mathematical content is more demanding.

How are the AS/A level assessed?

Assessment is broadly similar across the awarding bodies. AS level is assessed by two papers/components, ranging from 1½ to 1¾ hours, depending on the awarding body used. One of the exam papers at AS level includes questions on fieldwork completed. Examinations will include use of calculators where numerical data is being assessed. There are compulsory and optional elements and a mix of multi-choice, short answer and essay-based formats for questions. Eighty per cent of the final grade at A level is from examinations, 20% from a fieldwork study/investigation which must include primary (original data) collected by the student; the final report needs to be 3,000 to 4,000 words long. A level examinations range from 1½ to 2½ hours' duration, depending on the awarding body syllabus followed. There are two to three exam papers/components which can be a mix of multi-choice, short answer and essay-based formats. Questions are mostly compulsory although there are choices of questions in some examination sections or papers.

Combines well with

Geography combines well with sciences and art/humanities/social science subjects. There is some common ground with biology, geology, environmental science and physics from the sciences. Subjects such sociology, economics, government and politics and history fit well with the human aspects of geography. ***A level environmental science is sometimes considered too similar to geography for universities to count both subjects in the A level grade offers they make. Check institution requirements carefully.***

Recent A level results

Total students: 36,363 **(Male: 18,172, Female: 18,191)** **Overall pass rate: 99.0%**

A*	A	B	C	D	E	U
6.0	20.2	29.7	25.6	13.4	4.1	1.0

Higher education suitability

A facilitating subject and so well respected by universities for entry to a wide range of degree courses including business, politics, sociology, surveying, psychology, history, law, travel and tourism, geology, architecture and language based degrees, as long as other requirements are met.

Case study

Paul, from Essex, took geography as one of his A level subjects. He said:

'Geography was an obvious choice for me as I loved this subject at GCSE. It is a very varied subject at A level. There are scientific aspects such as interpreting hydrographs, geological topics, e.g. we looked at igneous, sedimentary and metamorphic rocks, and the human aspects as well, e.g. the different types of agriculture, industries and settlements we live in. There is some overlap with sociology in some respects. I was surprised at the mathematical modelling we covered, so you need a good grade in GCSE maths. There are so many issues these days that geography is relevant to, e.g. climate change, pollution and our effect on the environment and vice versa! The field trip we did in Year 12 lasted one week; I made the mistake of leaving it too long to write up my notes so one piece of advice I would give is to write up your notes and data day by day so you understand it later.'

Geography at university

A level geography will usually be required to study this subject as a degree. Geography is among the more popular degree subjects and so A level grade requirements can be high. One or two science subjects can also be required or among a list of preferred subjects at A level where the degree places a strong emphasis on physical geography.

Geography can be studied as a BA (Bachelor of Arts) or BSc (Bachelor of Science) degree, with the BA more focused on human aspects, the BSc on physical. Courses can vary considerably, and there are possibilities for specialising within the degree, e.g. marine geography, coastal geography, global development, environmental geography, hydrology, cartography or geomorphology. Fieldwork is an important component of a degree and field trips can be in the UK and/or abroad. Geography is widely available as a single subject or combined/joint degree, with many subject combinations at university possible. The more popular combinations with geography include environmental science/studies, sociology/anthropology, mathematics, economics or biology. Aspects of geography are relevant to agriculture and some agriculture-based degrees will either require or prefer geography as a subject at A level.

There are Foundation degree courses in subjects such as geography and the environment and geography and society, as well as land and environment subjects. HNC/D (Higher National Certificate or Diploma) environmental conservation management or geography are also available. Entry requirements for these qualifications are generally lower.

Jobs with A level geography

The skills developed from the study of geography are generally more important than the subject knowledge acquired. Geography is not a requirement for entry to the jobs listed here, but the skills developed are useful for: holiday courier/resort representative, freight forwarder, as well as a wide range of roles in business administration, finance and retail where good computer and team-working skills are required.

Graduate level jobs in geography

As with many degrees, geography develops certain ***skills*** that can be valuable to a wide range of occupations. The ability to research, analyse, interpret and classify data/information can be employed in occupational areas as diverse as from law to social work, and from banking/finance to recreational/leisure management, to name a few. Occupational areas where the subject matter in geography is particularly useful include:

- agriculture/horticulture
- cartography (map making)

- civil engineering
- environmentally related employment, e.g. recycling officers/hazard managers/ environmental campaigners – such roles involve working for organisations such as local authorities, utility companies or environmental charities/pressure groups
- journalism, especially writing for specialist magazines/journals
- logistics management – the transport and storage of goods
- surveying
- teaching
- town planning
- travel and tourism, e.g. eco tour guide, tour management.

Further reading

British Cartographic Society (BCS): www.cartography.org.uk

www.geography-site.co.uk

The Royal Geographical Society: www.rgs.org

Royal Institution of Chartered Surveyors (RICS): www.rics.org

Royal Town Planning Institute (RTPI): www.rtpi.org.uk

Geology

Geology is a field science that focuses on the structure, evolution and dynamics of the earth, and the exploration and extraction of mineral and energy resources within it, including oil, diamonds, uranium, sand and road stone. Minerals are essential for agricultural fertilisers, oil fuels our transport and provides a wealth of by-products that are used by industry and society. Geology draws on other subjects such as physics, chemistry, biology, geography and mathematics in its content and so an aptitude for these subjects will be required. The emphasis on the evolution of the Earth may prove a challenge to those with strong religious beliefs.

What do you study?

Precise content depends on the awarding body syllabus followed, but typical AS level content can include the following.

- Global tectonics: this involves the origin of the Earth and solar system, space exploration, meteorites, earthquakes, the theory of plate tectonics, the study of folds, faults and rock structures produced when rocks are deformed.
- The rock cycle: involves studying igneous, sedimentary and metamorphic rocks. The study of minerals and their identification. Volcanic eruptions, how sedimentary rocks form in deserts, rivers, glacial environments and how intense heat and pressure alters rocks by metamorphism.

A level will cover the above, plus the following.

- Evolution of the Earth, life and climate: this involves the study of how life originated and evolved; how fossils are preserved and how mass extinctions are caused. Dinosaurs and marine species such as trilobites and ammonites are also studied. Climate and sea level change over geological time will also form part of the syllabus.
- Economic geology: this studies the practical applications of geology, including:
  - how geology affects water resources and supply
  - energy resources, including oil exploration, coal mining and geothermal power
  - metal mineral resources, including formation of ores, prospecting and mining
  - engineering geology, including dams, sea defences and storage of nuclear waste

Courses will include visits to places of geological interest, e.g. Iceland, the Himalayas, Morocco, Wales, the Isle of Wight or Arran in Scotland. There is usually one field trip each year. Check with the college or sixth form you intend going to about the locations of field trips and what costs are involved.

Why study geology?

Geology heightens our awareness of the finite nature of natural resources and the need to find alternative sources of raw materials. The subject will be of particular interest to those who enjoy the study of fossils, dinosaurs, the causes of earthquakes and volcanic eruptions, as well as the practical applications of geology in modern society.

GCSE entry requirements

GCSE science at grade C/5 or above is usually required, and also mathematics. GCSE geography is useful but not a general requirement.

How different from GCSE?

More emphasis on applied aspects of geology and also greater depth of understanding of topics generally, especially scientific aspects where physics and chemistry are involved in geological processes.

How are the AS/A level assessed?

OCR is the only awarding body for this subject at AS and A level in England. AS level is assessed by one examination paper lasting 2½ hours. A level is assessed by three examination papers lasting between 1½ and 2¼ hours and a practical assessment covering a minimum of 12 specified skill areas. The practical is worth 22% of the total marks at A level.

Combines well with

Chemistry, physics, biology, environmental science.

Higher education suitability

Not a facilitating subject, but accepted for entry to a wide range of degree courses, as long as other requirements are met. Can be accepted as a science subject in some instances.

Geology at university

A level geology is not a usual requirement to study geology at univerity as it is not widely available. At least one science is advised, but two will maximise university options; check with institutions about particular requirements. There is some overlap with A level geography and so it is worth checking whether both subjects would be accepted for entry to a degree course.

At degree level, many universities offer courses in geology, geoscience or earth science. There are also specialist courses in subjects such as geophysics, geochemistry and engineering geology. Degrees are most commonly BSc, although there are MESci (Master of Environmental Science), MGeol (Master of Geology) and MSc (Master of Science) opportunities where an additional year of study leads to a postgraduate master's level qualification and an accepted step towards taking a PhD. There are no Foundation degree courses in geology but there are HNDs in construction and the built environment and HNCs in countryside and environmental management which include elements of geology. Geology as a degree can also be taken in combination with other subjects, most commonly geography, natural sciences and environmental science.

Case study

Andrew, from Hampshire, took A level geology alongside chemistry, physics and mathematics. He said:

> *'I took geology as I really enjoyed the physical aspects of geography at GCSE, and I was attracted to the scientific approach of geology which is much more in depth than the physical aspects of geography GCSE. Geology is a fascinating subject, especially the study of volcanic and seismic topics, and of course the stratigraphy and fossils which I had loved when I was a child. There is a lot to learn, especially the wide range of rocks, minerals and geological processes covered on the course. Field trips were really interesting, e.g. for one of ours we went to the Isle of Purbeck in Dorset, which has got all sorts of sedimentary rock features and plenty of fossils to find. Chemistry and physics support this subject, e.g. mineralogy and petrology. I would definitely recommend this subject if you are interested in the structure of the earth and how it evolved.'*

Jobs with A level geology

Geological technicians help and support the work of geoscientists. They look after the day-to-day running of the laboratory, setting up and monitoring experiments, analysing samples and survey results and managing equipment stocks. The scientific skills developed from A level geology could also be applied to other laboratory-based occupations. Museum assistant is also possible, e.g. where there are fossil collections. Aside from these, holding A levels generally can be useful for entry to a wide range of non-science/geology-based occupations, including business administration, finance, retail and customer service, where any subjects at A level are acceptable.

Graduate level jobs in geology

Particular occupations in which a degree in geology and closely related subjects are required include:

- engineering geologist
- environmental geologist
- geology teacher
- hydrogeologist
- minerals/mining geologist
- palaeontologist
- petroleum geologist
- research geologist/university lecturer.

Further reading

British Geological Survey (BGS): www.bgs.ac.uk

The Geological Society: www.geolsoc.org.uk

UK Fossils Network: www.ukfossils.co.uk

Government and politics

Politics has a direct effect on our lives as it directly affects areas such as our education, health, policing, defence and a wide range of other services at local and national levels. The outcomes of national and local elections determine priorities for public services, including the amount of taxes we pay. Politics is rarely, if ever, out of the news, with 2016 being a momentous year including the UK referendum vote to leave the European Union (Brexit), the election of Donald Trump as president of the USA, arguably one of the most controversial figures in US political history, and with a UK general election in 2017.

What do you study?

The precise content of courses depends on the awarding body specification followed by the sixth form or college you go to. AS and A level government and politics cover the study of how governments and political systems work in countries such as the UK and the USA. At AS level, students gain a broad understanding of the political system in the UK which covers the role of general and local elections, political parties and pressure groups such as trade unions and groups that represent particular causes, e.g. the environment, housing or prison reform.

Concepts such as democracy and citizenship are studied, as well as the institutions of British government: Parliament, the executive (elected government and the civil service) and the judiciary (law courts) and how they relate to each other. The WJEC (Welsh Joint Education Committee) Eduqas syllabus includes study of government in modern Wales. A level presents students with options which may include the study of politics in the USA. In the new specification there is an option to study global politics.

Particular issues may be studied, e.g. race and ethnic politics, religion in politics, the European Union, education, the environment, globalisation and rights and freedoms. Ideologies such as conservatism, socialism, social democracy, liberalism, fascism, feminism and nationalism can also be studied, as well as concepts such as power, democracy, rights and freedoms.

Government and politics is taught through lessons, but courses can include visits to places such as Parliament and/or political organisations. Guest speakers may be invited and debates, discussions and/or mock elections conducted are likely to be a part of the course.

Why study government and politics?

Government and politics enables students to think analytically and present reasoned arguments effectively. These are useful skills for a wide range of careers, including those in business, law, journalism and teaching. The decision to take AS/A level government and politics should be based on ***interest in the subject, not on future career aims***. It is NOT a requirement to have studied the subject at A level for entry to a degree course in politics at university, but it will give some insight into it. Government and politics will appeal to students who enjoy discussions, debates and current affairs.

GCSE entry requirements

GCSE English language at grade C/5 or above generally required, as government and politics is an essay-based subject. GCSEs in humanities subjects such as history, geography or religious studies are useful but by no means a general requirement.

How different from GCSE?

Not widely available at GCSE, although aspects are covered in citizenship, e.g. human rights and government systems. AS and A level require much greater POLITICAL analysis and essays are longer. Also much wider reading is required, including quality newspapers.

How are the AS/A level assessed?

AQA and Pearson Edexcel are the two awarding bodies in England for this subject. The AQA AS level is assessed by one examination paper lasting 3 hours, and A level is assessed by three examinations, each lasting 2 hours. Pearson Edexcel AS level is assessed by two examination papers, each lasting 1¾ hours and A level by three examinations, each lasting 2 hours. All comprise essay and medium-length response-type questions. There is some choice over questions answered.

Combines well with

History, law, sociology, English, economics, religious studies, geography and philosophy. Subjects like these can help students to understand the contexts within which government and political institutions operate and the constraints and challenges which governments encounter. A modern language would be useful or even required if you are aiming to study overseas as part of a degree programme.

Recent A level results

Total students: 15,540 **(Male: 8,500, Female: 7,040)** **Overall pass rate: 98.2%**

A*	A	B	C	D	E	U
6.5	20.7	29.2	23.9	12.8	5.1	1.8

Case study

Kevin, from Essex, took A levels in government and politics, history and sociology. He said:

> *'You really need to be interested in politics and current affairs generally to enjoy this subject. Lessons were really lively, with lots of discussions and we had a trip to Parliament which was very interesting. I was amazed at how small the chambers of the House of Commons and House of Lords are! History A level helped me understand politics better, as in history we learned about the development of political parties in Britain in the 19th and 20th centuries. To do well in government and politics you really need to read quality newspapers such as The Times or Guardian regularly as they keep you up to date with current events and affairs. Essays also need to be properly structured, as you have to present well-written arguments about particular topics.'*

Higher education suitability

Not a facilitating subject, but accepted for entry to most degree subjects, as long as other requirements are met.

Politics at university

Universities do not generally specify A level subjects, although some have preferred subjects, which can be the facilitating AS/A levels or others such as sociology, law, economics or philosophy.

There is a diversity of politics degrees, so check content carefully! These can include: international relations, politics of the third world/developing countries, Western liberal democracies, e.g. Canada, USA, European democracies, British politics, elections, political ideologies, political theory.

Politics can be combined with subjects such as law, economics, languages, history, sociology, international relations, social policy or philosophy, but other combinations are possible. Some courses can include working or studying abroad as part of the course, e.g. to observe the work of major governmental/political organisations such as the European Commission or NATO (the North Atlantic Treaty Organisation).

At undergraduate level politics is available only as a degree. There are HNC/D (Higher National Certificate or Diploma) and Foundation degree courses in subjects such as public services, police studies or legal studies which include elements of government and politics.

Jobs with A level government and politics

AS/A level government and politics are NOT required for the following occupations, but would be useful. Examples include: civil service and local government e.g. in administrative roles; uniformed public service employment, e.g. the police, prison service, fire service; as well as working for charities or pressure groups, e.g. trade unions, environmental or housing issue organisations. Political parties employ a range of staff, e.g. those in administrative and finance roles to run party offices.

Graduate level jobs in government and politics

A politics degree is by no means required for entry into the following jobs, but would be an advantage.

- **Civil servant:** senior-level civil servants advise government ministers.
- **Elected politicians:** although few will have actually studied this subject.
- **Lobbyists and consultants:** people who are recruited by businesses or pressure groups that want particular issues/causes raised and examined in Parliament.
- **Local government officers:** work for local authorities (councils) in the provision of services, e.g. education, highways, social services. Local authorities also employ a range of professionals, e.g. architects, surveyors, lawyers, social workers and teachers.
- **Political agents or researchers.**
- **Working for international organisations:** e.g. the United Nations. For certain roles, language graduates may be required.

There are also a range of jobs which involve contact with politics, including journalism, working for trade unions, charities or academic research in universities.

The skills learned from the study of government and politics include oral and written self-expression and researching information effectively, which are widely transferable into many occupations.

Further reading

Civil Service careers: www.civilservice.gov.uk/jobs

GOV.UK – UK government services and information: www.gov.uk

Trades Union Congress (TUC): www.tuc.org.uk

UK Parliament: www.parliament.uk

History

The study of history involves gathering facts and evidence from the past and interpreting them in order to uncover patterns and meanings. It is often said that without the past we are simply unable to see or understand the present. Events from the past, which include the daily routines of individuals through to momentous happenings that affected the whole world, are in themselves just a jumble of unrelated phenomena. 'History' is the attempt to make some sort of sense out of this apparent chaos and give a viable perspective on it.

Historians will use written evidence as their main source of reference through study of a wide range of historical documents, including literature, parish records, written laws and newspapers, in addition to ancient artefacts found at archaeological excavations. The study of history is not merely the learning by rote of key dates and names of past notable individuals; it is also about comprehending a whole process that gives us some understanding of the present and our place in it and the future.

What do you study?

There are many course specifications available in history, so for course content check with the sixth form or college you intend going to. The subject enables you to study from a wide range of countries/historical periods/topics, e.g. the 'Troubles' in Ireland, the Crusades, the USA and Vietnam 1961–75, Germany, the Soviet Union under Stalin, Italy, China, France, the Tudor and Stuart periods in England or the English Civil War. A level now requires that students study British history and topics generally from a chronological period of not less than 200 years. There can be visits to places of historical interest.

Why study history?

The study of history will provide you with skills that can be used in a wide range of occupations. The ability to read and research information effectively and to present well-structured and argued written work is readily transferable to a wide range of university subjects and occupations, with notable examples including law, journalism, public relations, business, management and social sciences such as economics, sociology and psychology.

GCSE entry requirements

GCSE English language at grade C/5 or above is a general requirement, owing to the written demands of history at AS and A level. GCSE history is not always essential but may be preferred, to show evidence of interest in the subject. If history GCSE was taken, a grade C/5 or above will probably be required.

How different from GCSE?

AS and A level rely on your ability to use information sources a lot more. Essays will be longer and need to demonstrate a greater depth of understanding than at GCSE. You will also probably need to make more contribution to class discussions. There is a lot of individual study, mostly reading around the subject to strengthen your knowledge. This is ESSENTIAL if higher grades are to be achieved. The topics covered can be different from GCSE, so make sure that you know what is on offer at the college or sixth form you intend on going to.

How are the AS/A level assessed?

In England, AS levels across the awarding bodies comprise two examination papers, ranging from 1½ to 2¼ hours' duration, depending on the awarding body, with one paper covering British and the other non-British history. At A level, across the awarding bodies in England there are typically two or three examinations accounting for 80% of the total marks; a written assignment set by the school/college and ranging from 3,000 to 4,000 words in length accounts for 20%. Examinations will have optional questions and in some cases a compulsory question must be answered.

Combines well with

English literature, government and politics, law, sociology, economics and modern foreign or classical languages are especially good combinations with history. All develop writing skills and researching information effectively and critically, which are essential skills for the study of history. History can also be used as a third A level or fourth subject at AS level for entry to science-based degrees, including medicine, dentistry and veterinary science/medicine.

Recent A level results

Total students: 54,731 **(Male: 25,252, Female: 29,479)** **Overall pass rate: 99.4%**

A*	A	B	C	D	E	U
5.4	18.0	31.9	28.0	14.5	3.6	0.6

Higher education suitability

As a facilitating subject, history is highly respected by all universities for entry to a variety of courses. It is a good subject for progression into social science and humanities courses at university, such as history, English, law, sociology and economics. However, it is by no means restricted to being useful for these courses. Indeed many leading universities also respect science students for taking history, as the analytical and writing skills gained from it are invaluable in any field. History is therefore a good subject as an AS or A level for students thinking of studying medicine or single sciences at university.

Case study

Anthony took A levels in history, law and politics at a school sixth form. He said about history A level:

> *'I love history, so for me it was an obvious subject to choose. What helps is to have an enthusiastic teacher and ours were brilliant (we had two teachers to cover the areas needed). My course included the study of Russia/the USSR 1881 to 1951, which I found fascinating. There is a lot of political stuff covered in this, e.g. Bolshevism/Communism, so there is some similarity with parts of A level politics. A level history is much harder than GCSE and you also have to do a LOT more reading to get the higher marks and grades. I did GCSE history but it isn't essential to have taken it, as the A level covers different topics. You need to be able to source the right information and to read well, which are more to do with English language than history. Essays can take ages to write, so you need to be someone who is prepared to put in the work and enjoys writing.'*

History at university

A level history is not always required, although it is advisable to take it to demonstrate interest and motivation to study the subject to degree level. For entry to more competitive entry universities, a second facilitating subject is recommended. GCSE in a modern foreign language can be required for entry to some degree courses in history. Visits to historical sites can enhance a university application and demonstrate an active interest in the subject, as well as watching historical documentaries/programmes on TV and other media and reading magazines such as *History Today*.

There are many areas that can be studied which may not have been encountered at A level. These include social history of medicine, religious history, gender history, peace studies, economic and social history, North American history or medieval history. British and/or European history are the most commonly covered topics but they vary in the time periods studied. History at university can also be combined with many other subjects, including government and politics, sociology, geography, theology, geography and languages, as well as sciences. Some history-based degrees, especially modern history courses, can include one year studying or working in a country that is being studied.

There are Foundation degrees in subjects such as heritage management, historical building conservation, archaeology or historic garden management and restoration. Entry requirements are generally lower than for a degree, with a minimum of one subject having been passed at A level (in many cases history) and at least one other studied but not necessarily passed at A level. Note that this is the general minimum for entry to a Foundation degree and individual college or university requirements can be higher.

Jobs with A level history

Jobs working in areas such as libraries or archives at assistant level are possible, but the skills developed from taking A level history can be readily transferred to a much wider range of employment, e.g. journalism (although most journalists are university graduates), marketing, sales, customer service and business administration, all of which require people who can express themselves well orally or in writing.

Graduate level jobs in history

There are not many occupations which involve directly working in history, but there are many more where the skills developed from studying the subject can be usefully employed. Examples of occupations directly working in history where a degree is usually required are:

- archaeologist
- archivist
- genealogist
- museum curator
- teaching – at primary, secondary, further and higher education levels
- working for organisations such as English Heritage or the National Trust, e.g. as an education officer/guide.

As with A level, the skills developed from studying history can be readily transferred to a wide range of occupational areas.

Further reading

Council for British Archaeology: new.archaeologyuk.org

Historical Association: www.history.org.uk

History Today: www.historytoday.com

Museums Association: www.museumsassociation.org

History of art

This subject involves the study of the works of artists, sculptors and architects. Traditionally the focus has been on those in the Western world, Europe in particular, but the new specification by Pearson Edexcel (the only awarding body to offer A level) is much more diverse, covering work by men, women and a range of racial groups and cultures. Works are studied in the context in which they were created, i.e. the political, religious, social, economic and cultural influences on the creators, the traditions in which they worked and the techniques used in painting, sculpture and architecture. History of Art is offered as an A level only.

What do you study?

The new specification content covers three areas:

- visual analysis
- themes
- periods.

For visual analysis, students develop analytical skills across painting, sculpture and architecture by studying the European tradition of art from classical Greece (500 BC) to the present. This core skill will enable students to analyse artists' work to identify more complex interdependencies between visual language and the effects achieved.

Two themes must be selected from a list of three:

- nature in art and architecture
- identities in art and architecture
- war in art and architecture.

Students explore artists and works from both pre- and post-1850 and both within and beyond the European tradition. They must study work across at least three types of art: two- and three-dimensional, e.g. painting and sculpture, and architecture. Examples of artists and architects studied include: Monet, Turner, O'Keefe and Dürer (painters), Flanagan, Hepworth, Long and Giambologna (sculptors) and Nash, Gaudi, Lloyd Wright and Galatrava (architects), but far more than these are studied.

An additional six works are also studied and these must include at least three from outside of Europe, e.g. China, Turkey, India, Australasia and the Americas.

History of art also covers study of the political, cultural, social and technological contexts in which works of art were produced and deals with issues such as sexuality, social class, ethnicity and patriarchy.

Two periods from the following five are chosen for the periods aspect of the A level:

- invention and illusion: the Renaissance in Italy (1420–1520)
- power and persuasion: the Baroque in Catholic Europe (1597–1685)
- rebellion and revival: the British and French Avant-Garde (1848–99)
- brave new world: Modernism in Europe (1900–39)
- pop life: British and American contemporary art and architecture (1960–2015).

This subject is based on detailed study of works of art, and so there will be a lot of group-based activity such as discussion of images of paintings, sculptures and buildings. There are also visits to galleries in the UK and in some cases to European centres such as Paris, Florence or Barcelona. With the new specifications, visits to the wider world could be included. Check with the sixth form or college you intend going to for details.

Why study history of art?

This is a subject that develops skills in analysing visual images by looking at the style and content of works of art. Students are encouraged to develop their opinions and express them through written essays and class discussions. These skills complement those developed by other subjects listed below. These skills are also useful for employment where the abilities to observe well and communicate effectively are required.

GCSE entry requirements

There is no GCSE in history of art, but subjects such as art and design, photography, religious studies, languages (ancient or modern) or history can help to provide some understanding of history of art. GCSE English language at grade C/5 or above will likely be required, owing to the written requirements of history of art.

How are the AS/A level assessed?

The A level will be assessed by two examination papers, each lasting 3 hours and each contributing 50% towards the final marks and grade awarded. The examinations include a visual analysis of a painting, a building and a sculpture, and a choice of questions covering nature in art and architecture, identities in art and architecture and war in art and architecture. Also included in the examinations are the periods of study listed above, where students answer questions based on two of the five areas available. There are compulsory and optional questions in both examination papers.

Combines well with

This depends on whether you wish to study history of art at university, in which case A levels in art and design, English literature, history, classical civilisation and modern languages all provide useful knowledge and study skills. If you are intending to study archaeology at university, sciences combine well with history of art.

Case study

Ana Rose is taking history of art as one of her A level subjects. She said:

> *'I chose history of art because I have always been interested not only in how an artwork has been executed, but in how art has changed ever since prehistory and why. I always believed that through this subject, I will be able to get an insight into how society was like in the previous periods, how people used art to confront issues and how art has been used as a medium to express emotions. People leave a mark on Earth through art, and studying history of art allowed me to learn and understand the concepts and philosophies behind various artistic movements, lessons which have influenced the way I think and the way I question things. It is sometimes challenging to understand certain artworks and movements, which is completely normal. History of art can be considered a tough subject but it feels quite rewarding once you complete your assignments and hand in your written work (essays, mostly), because not only have you finished a task, but you have also learned something new, something that will shape the way you think about artworks. Make notes! Bring a small sketchbook wherever you go to note down everything you find interesting in the streets and in galleries. Question things, never conform. Try to understand the pieces of writing that your teacher gives you and make sure to ask questions because this will help you to further understand what you're reading about. Also, make sure to have a small notebook to note down all the words which are unfamiliar to you. This will be very handy when writing your essays! In terms of producing practical outcomes, make sure to explore as many ideas as possible through diagrams and never stick to just one concept, no matter how solid you think this may be.'*

Higher education suitability

Not a facilitating subject, but acceptable for entry to almost any university subject, as long as other requirements are met.

History of art at university

It is not a requirement to have taken this subject at A level in order to study it at degree level, largely because it is not offered at many colleges and schools with sixth forms. Having taken it will demonstrate interest in the subject, which can enhance a university application. Most universities are open about subjects studied at A level, although subjects such as art and design, English literature or history can be among preferred or even required subjects in some instances. If a course involves practical art, then A level art and design or even a Diploma in Foundation Studies may be required where a portfolio needs to be produced.

University courses can be broader in scope and not restricted to Western art in their focus. Some courses can involve practical studio work, others involve studying abroad, including Australia (Aboriginal art) and North America (Native American art). Time spent abroad can be anything from a few weeks to a full year.

There are many possibilities and combinations available with history of art, including history and philosophy of art, art history and practice, comparative literature, liberal arts, Central and East European studies, Arabic and modern foreign languages, to name a few.

There are no Foundation degree courses in art history, although some courses will include a module in the subject. There are many Foundation degree and HNC/D (Higher National Certificate or Diploma) courses in practical/applied subjects in the creative industries, including games design, fine art, illustration, graphics and contemporary fine art practice. See the entry on art and design for more information (pages 24–27).

Jobs with A level history of art

There can be jobs and apprenticeships where a knowledge of art history is needed or useful. Examples include working for antiques dealers, furniture restorers, auction houses and galleries. Employment would probably be in the capacity of an assistant in the first instance. Also, jobs in the heritage sector working for organisations such as the National Trust, English Heritage or museums may be possible. A level history of art is unlikely to be required for entry to any of these but it would give some useful background knowledge and understanding of techniques and materials. Aside from these, there are higher and degree apprenticeships where any A level subjects are acceptable for entry, e.g. in administration, management and customer service.

Graduate level jobs in history of art

For jobs at this level, postgraduate study and training is likely to be needed, e.g. as in the case of archives, librarianship or journalism (broadcast or written). Examples of graduate level occupations which involve working with or at least having contact with history of art include:

- archaeologist, especially conservation and restoration work
- archivist
- arts administrator
- auctioneer or valuer
- librarian
- specialist roles in the travel and tourism industry, e.g. education officer or tour guide talking on art tours
- teaching in sixth form or college
- university lecturing.

Aside from the above, there are many careers where any degree subject is acceptable for entry, including a wide range of business and finance-based occupations, the civil service and local government.

Further reading

Association for Art History: www.forarthistory.org.uk

The Institute of Conservation: www.icon.org.uk

Law

More accurately described as General Principles of English Law (Scotland has a different legal system and law professionals), the study of law involves learning about how the rules by which we live are created, developed and administered. The subject includes a requirement for students to apply their knowledge of law to solve cases given.

What do you study?

The subject involves investigation of a variety of areas including the following.

- Where our laws come from (sources of law) and how they are made – Acts of Parliament, European law (a prominent issue following the June 2016 referendum that resulted in the UK choosing to leave the European Union), custom and precedent (rulings by judges).
- How disputes are resolved – the criminal and civil courts, tribunals and arbitration.
- The functions of law, e.g. protection of rights and freedoms.
- The personnel of law, e.g. judges, magistrates, barristers, solicitors.
- Criminal law, including offences against the person, e.g. murder, manslaughter, offences against property, e.g. theft, robbery, burglary, and defences that may be raised by the accused in criminal prosecutions.
- Civil law, including the law of 'torts' (the French for 'wrongs'), e.g. negligence, trespass, nuisance, defamation of character, occupier's liability, and the law of contract – how contracts are formed, contracts that are invalid, remedies for the successful claimant.

AS and A level courses are classroom based, although there can be visits to places like law courts to get an insight into the law in action.

Why study law?

Law develops skills in analytical thinking, making reasoned judgements and understanding the consequences of these. Such skills are also very useful in higher-level study of social sciences such as psychology or sociology, business and also other essay-based subjects such as English, politics, history or classics. The choice of studying law at A level should be based on interest in the subject rather than future career plans, as it is not a requirement to have taken it at A level for entry to a law degree or other higher education qualification in law. Having A level law does have some advantage when applying for non-graduate occupations in law, such as legal executive (see below).

GCSE entry requirements

GCSE English language at grade C/5 or above is usually specified.

How different from GCSE?

GCSE law is not a widely taken subject, but AS and A level rely on your ability to use information sources a lot more. A much wider range of case law is covered and there is more in-depth analysis of topics such as crime, contract and torts. Written assignments will be longer and need to demonstrate a greater depth of understanding than at GCSE. You will also probably need to make more contribution to class discussions. There is a lot of individual study, with much more reading around the subject to strengthen your knowledge.

How are the AS/A level assessed?

Law is assessed 100% by examination, and across the awarding bodies in England it is very similar. AS level is assessed by two examination papers, each lasting 1½ hours and comprising multi-choice, short answer and essay-based questions. A level is assessed by three examination papers, each lasting 2 hours and comprising multi-choice, short answer and essay-based questions.

Combines well with

Essay-based subjects such as English literature, English language or history, as these develop skills in oral and written self-expression. Business studies or economics can help you to understand the context in which law operates; sociology, psychology or government and politics can also give a basis for the study of law-related subjects. A modern foreign language can be very useful or even a requirement if you are aiming to study at university in another country. Science subjects at A level can be useful if you want to specialise later in areas such as intellectual property, e.g. patenting.

Recent A level results

Total students: 11,272 **(Male: 4,119, Female: 7,153)** **Overall pass rate: 96.4%**

A*	A	B	C	D	E	U
4.3	12.8	25.5	26.3	18.6	8.9	3.6

Higher education suitability

Not a facilitating subject, but widely accepted as an A level subject for entry to a broad range of university courses, as long as other requirements are met.

Case study

Anthony, from a school sixth form, said about A level law:

'There are LOTS of cases to learn for this subject and you need to apply these to the questions you get in exams. What helped us a lot was that our tutor gave us past exam papers to try out and this really helped develop good technique and a much better idea of the sort of information needed for good answers. You really do need to read and understand the textbooks given, and also to keep up to date with what is going on in the world of law by reading good quality papers like The Times, which contains law reports. Essays need to be clear and well structured, so you need a good level of English language for this A level. There is a lot to learn and there is much more to law than just high-level criminal cases and courtrooms. I was very surprised to learn that most criminal cases (about 90%) are tried in magistrates' courts, for example. There is a bit of overlap with government and politics, as in law you learn about where laws come from such as Acts of Parliament and European law, some of which is covered in politics A level.'

Law at university

Some universities prefer students to start their law degree as a beginner to the subject. I have heard one admissions tutor from a Russell Group university say: 'Having A level law is neither an advantage nor disadvantage for entry to a law degree.' A comment that has been made by some universities is that taking the A level can lead to complacency in the first year at university at least, or to the wrong kind of understanding of the subject. Two facilitating A level subjects should be taken, with at least one subject being essay based, especially if you are aiming to get into the more competitive entry universities. In addition to qualification requirements, some universities use an admissions test called LNAT (National Admissions Test for Law) to assess applicants' suitability to study law at degree level. Activities such as visiting a law court and reading books such as *Understanding the Law* by Geoffrey Rivlin and *Learning the Law* by Glanville Williams will enhance your understanding of law and your university application.

Law can be studied as a single subject or joint/combined with another subject or subjects. The degree needs to cover the foundations of legal knowledge in order for students to obtain maximum exemption from professional examinations to qualify as a barrister or solicitor later. The foundations that must be covered are:

- contract (also known as obligations)
- criminal law
- equity and the law of trusts
- European law
- property law
- public law
- tort (also known as obligations).

Additional options can be taken, such as employment law, family law, tax law and commercial (company) law. Some law degrees will include the LPC (Legal Practice Certificate) for solicitors or a 'Bar Exempting' course for barristers. Related university subjects include criminology and human rights and criminal justice, which are useful for entry to careers in the police, prison or probation services. Law can combine with many other subjects at university, including politics, economics, sociology, business and languages. Law and a language are particularly useful, as study of international law addresses the increasing requirement for lawyers to operate internationally.

There are HNC/D (Higher National Certificate or Diploma) and Foundation degree courses available in more vocational subjects such as business law, legal practice, legal studies and police studies. Entry requirements are generally lower than for a degree but such qualifications can be useful as an entry to work such as paralegal, legal executive or police service.

Jobs with A level law

A level law can give some exemption from parts of the legal executive (CILEX) qualifications. This sort of work can be entered through apprenticeships and also through paralegal and legal secretarial work. Outside of law careers, the skills developed from taking the A level can be usefully employed in business administration, customer service and marketing roles, where an ability to express oneself well is required.

Graduate level jobs in law

To become a law professional, further study and training will be required. The main professions in England and Wales are:

- barrister
- solicitor
- legal executive
- conveyancer
- paralegal.

A law degree is not a requirement to enter any of the above, including barrister and solicitor, but where another degree subject has been taken a postgraduate law conversion course such as a Common Professional Exam or Postgraduate Diploma in Law will be required before you enter training for barrister or solicitor. A law degree will give quicker entry to postgraduate training.

Further reading

All About Law: www.allaboutlaw.co.uk

www.lawcareers.net

National Admissions Test for Law: www.lnat.ac.uk

Mathematics F / Further mathematics F / Statistics

There are three types of mathematics at A level:

- mathematics
- further mathematics
- statistics.

Mathematics generally is a subject that, to a greater or lesser extent, forms the foundation for others, including physics, chemistry, economics, business, psychology, biology and computer science. Mathematics is used to describe and predict a wide range of things, e.g. the speed of a chemical reaction, rate of acceleration of vehicles, planetary motion, the ways decisions are made in business and the behaviour of large groups of people. It is a demanding subject at AS and A level, necessitating a high level of understanding rather than extensive knowledge, and the ability to think logically and work things out.

Further mathematics is a very advanced course of pure and applied mathematics, in the latter case covering statistics, mechanics and decision mathematics. These topics are covered in even greater depth than those encountered in A level mathematics.

Statistics is the study of the collection, analysis, interpretation, presentation and organisation of data. Statistics can be applied to a wide range of things, e.g. scientific, industrial or social problems. It is usual to begin with a statistical population or a statistical model process to be studied. Populations can be diverse topics such as 'all people living in a country' or 'every atom composing a crystal'. Statistics deals with all aspects of data, including the planning of data collection in terms of the design of surveys and research.

What do you study?

Mathematics and further mathematics, or mathematics and statistics are studied together but are treated as separate subjects for university entry. UCAS tariff points achieved for both subjects are counted.

Mathematics will comprise the following.

- Pure mathematics: algebra, trigonometry, vectors, graphs, calculus, co-ordinate geometry, functions, numerical methods, logarithms, exponentials, linear and quadratic equations. Pure mathematics underpins other areas covered as below.

- Mechanics: this is essentially the description of how objects move in distance, speed, acceleration and time and how these are related. Also covered are the action of force on stationary and moving objects, momentum and energy, vectors and circulatory and oscillatory motion. These feature strongly in other subjects such as physics, engineering, physical geography/geology and architecture.
- Decision mathematics: ideas behind decision making in applied business situations. This involves network diagrams, linear programming, route inspection problems, critical path analysis and algorithms. These also feature in economics and computer science.

Further mathematics will typically cover:

- Pure mathematics, comprising algebra, calculus, trigonometry, geometry, vectors and numerical methods. These will include concepts such as scalar and cross product of vectors applied to three-dimensional space, different co-ordinate systems and solutions of a range of differential equations, hyperbolic functions, matrices and mathematical induction.
- Mechanics, comprising relative motion, collisions, more complex motion in one dimension, stability, application of vectors in mechanics, variable mass, moments of inertia of a rigid body and rotation of a rigid body.
- Decision mathematics, comprising algorithms, algorithms on graphs, critical path analysis, the route inspection problem, linear programming, matchings and flows in networks.
- Statistics, comprising the binomial and Poisson distributions, continuous random variables, continuous distributions, samples and hypothesis tests.

Statistics AS level will cover:

- processes
- data presentation probability
- discrete random variables
- the binomial distribution and its use in hypothesis testing
- probability models
- Poisson distribution
- normal distribution
- sample data: estimation and hypothesis testing
- sampling design of experiments
- estimation and hypothesis testing
- correlation.

Statistics A level will cover:

- numerical measures, graphs and diagrams
- probability
- population and samples
- introduction to probability distributions
- binomial distribution
- normal distribution
- correlation and linear regression
- Bayes' theorem

- probability distributions
- experimental design
- exponential and Poisson distribution
- correlation and linear regression
- introduction to hypothesis testing
- contingency tables
- 1 and 2 sample non-parametric tests
- experimental design
- sampling, estimates and resampling
- hypothesis testing, significance testing, confidence intervals and power
- hypothesis testing for 1 and 2 samples
- paired tests
- goodness of fit
- analysis of variance
- effect size.

Students will need a calculator that has statistical functions, but no particular software knowledge is expected to join the course.

Typically, mathematics, further mathematics and statistics AS and A levels will involve the teacher/lecturer introducing new material and then working through example problems with the whole group listening and watching. Students are then expected to tackle problems themselves and these become increasingly complex. This will involve use of pen and paper, but scientific calculators will be used. Computer modelling will also be employed to model systems and work with larger-scale problems. Aside from lessons, students will need to practise outside of class and to allocate about six hours per week ***minimum*** to this. It is ESSENTIAL to keep up with work, as falling behind can make it difficult to catch up, given the continuous nature of the subject. The techniques of one topic need to be fully grasped and understood before progression to the next. Students must therefore be self-disciplined and highly motivated; those who rely solely on lessons will at best achieve a poor grade, and more likely fail.

Owing to the very high level of mathematical skills required, group sizes in AS and A level further mathematics tend to be small, and so there is more interaction with the teacher than in many other subjects.

Why study mathematical subjects?

Mathematics is one of the most employable subjects; the skills developed from studying it are highly valued by employers, e.g. the ability to solve complex problems and to work systematically and methodically. There is much evidence to demonstrate that people with higher-level numerical skills have a generally higher level of earning potential than others.

Further mathematics is usually required to take a maths degree and some other strongly number-based subjects, e.g. engineering or economics. Grade requirements can be HIGH.

Statistics is a useful subject for university courses in which statistics can feature, e.g. psychology, sociology, business studies, economics, sciences or geography. Statistics can be taken as a second subject by AS/A level mathematics students or by others who want to take a numerate subject to a higher level than GCSE but not cover all the topics encountered on AS and A level mathematics. It is also useful for apprenticeships in occupational areas such as accounting, banking and finance.

GCSE entry requirements

GCSE mathematics at grade A/7 is commonly required. Some colleges/ sixth forms may accept a grade B/6 but some require such applicants to sit some form of mathematics assessment to ascertain their level of competence in the subject. For further mathematics, GCSE grade A*/8 or 9 is usually required.

How different from GCSE?

Mathematics is a continuous subject and so AS and A level follow on from topics introduced at GCSE, although new topics will be encountered. The main difference is the depth of understanding required, with AS and A level dealing with far more complex problems than those encountered at GCSE. AS level statistics will build on statistical topics covered in GCSE mathematics or statistics. Topics such as calculus do not generally appear in AS level statistics.

How are the AS/A level assessed?

At the time of writing, the specifications for all three subjects are in draft format. All will likely be 100% assessed by examination. Mathematics AS level will be assessed by two examination papers covering pure and applied mathematics, lasting 2 hours and 1 hour, respectively. A level will be assessed by three examination papers comprising two pure mathematics papers lasting 2 hours each and one applied mathematics lasting 1 hour. All questions are compulsory (further mathematics does have optional questions on AS and A level papers). Scientific calculators can be used on certain papers but not on others.

Further mathematics AS level will be assessed by two examinations, comprising a pure mathematics paper and an optional topics choice paper where students choose ONE topic from pure mathematics, decision mathematics, statistics and mechanics on which to answer questions; examinations last 1½ hours. The A level will be assessed by up to four examination papers, comprising two pure mathematics papers and two papers covering optional topics where students choose ONE topic from pure mathematics, decision mathematics, statistics or mechanics on which to answer questions. A level papers last 1½ hours each.

AS level statistics will be assessed by two examination papers, each lasting 1½ hours and each contributing 50% towards the final marks and grade.

A level statistics will be assessed by three examination papers, each lasting 2 hours and each contributing 33.3% towards the final marks and grades.

Combines well with

Physics, chemistry, computer science, economics and psychology. Topics encountered in A levels in geography, biology, sociology and business can be well supported by topics such as statistics that are taken in mathematics, or by statistics itself. In fact, mathematics can be combined with any other subjects at AS or A level. Mathematics is taken alongside further mathematics A level, but the two are treated as separate qualifications and so both give UCAS Tariff points.

Recent A level results (mathematics)

Total students: 92,163 **(Male: 56,535, Female: 35,628)** **Overall pass rate: 97.1%**

A*	A	B	C	D	E	U
17.5	24.3	22.3	16.1	10.8	6.1	2.9

Recent A level results (further mathematics)

Total students: 15,257 **(Male: 11,054, Female: 4,203)** **Overall pass rate: 98.1%**

A*	A	B	C	D	E	U
28.7	27.5	20.6	11.3	6.5	3.5	1.9

Higher education suitability

Mathematics and further mathematics are facilitating subjects, and so are universally accepted for entry to university, as long as other requirements are met.

Case study

Luke, from John Cleveland Sixth Form in Leicestershire, is taking A level biology, chemistry and mathematics. Concerning mathematics, he said:

> *'I enjoy mathematics and all the different aspects of it. I also feel that I'm good at maths, which helps. The work is a lot harder than the maths covered at GCSE and you really need to concentrate in lessons. Also, it is very important to go through extra questions outside of lessons and practise going over methods. You need to enjoy and be good at this subject and to keep up with the work needed. You need to be able to understand one topic before you move on to the next.'*

Mathematics/statistics at university

A level mathematics is a requirement for entry to a degree in these subjects, and in many cases further mathematics will also be required for a mathematics degree. Expect a high grade requirement. ***Students considering taking a gap year after A levels need to check with universities on how they view this. Some may be concerned about loss of study continuity and may require students to take a summer school in mathematics before starting university (these are sometimes offered). Others may not permit a gap year at all.*** Extra activities such as entering mathematics competitions, playing chess or joining mathematics clubs all add value to a university application and demonstrate interest and motivation. The book *How to Solve It* by Polya is worth reading.

There are BSc (Bachelor of Science) degrees and also the MMath degree, in which the 'M' stands for 'master', but this is in fact an undergraduate degree. The MMath usually involves an initial 2 years of study which are the same for the BSc, and then a further 2 to 3 years' study of more demanding topics. This provides a very good foundation for postgraduate study leading to MSci (Master of Science) or PhD qualifications. The decision whether to take the BSc or MMath pathway usually depends on performance in the first 2 years at university, with more able students opting for the latter. As with the continuation from GCSE to A level, a degree will follow on from topics studied at A level, but the content becomes more abstract and difficult to relate to everyday life situations. University courses vary but may focus on areas such as pure mathematics, mathematical physics, discrete mathematics, financial mathematics or engineering mathematics. In addition, mathematics education can be studied, which leads to a teaching qualification as well as a degree in mathematics.

Aside from degrees, there are also Foundation degrees in subjects such as education and training for mathematics; these can be taken by those wanting to work as numeracy specialist teaching assistants. There are also HNC/D (Higher National Certificate or Diploma) courses in mathematics and computing. Other Foundation degree and HNC/D courses that include mathematics include engineering, accounting, business and information technology.

Statistics can be studied as a single subject or combined with others, e.g. mathematics, or may feature prominently on other courses including management, actuarial science, data analytics, finance, economics and psychology. There are opportunities to study or work abroad on a 'sandwich' basis as part of the degree.

There are also DipHE (Diploma of Higher Education), Foundation degree and HND courses which include statistics, e.g. business, management or mathematical sciences.

Jobs with A level mathematics/further mathematics/statistics

There are many advanced, higher and (increasingly) degree apprenticeships in occupations where mathematics features prominently. These include accounting, banking, engineering and computing. However, the skills learned from study of mathematics at A level can be readily transferred to other areas of work, including the civil service, local government or retail management. All can benefit from the logical thinking and problem-solving skills that mathematicians develop.

Graduate level jobs in mathematics/further mathematics/statistics

Mathematics is valued in a wide range of careers far beyond those considered to be numerically based. Examples of graduate level occupational areas in which mathematics is used extensively include:

- accountancy
- actuarial science
- computer programming
- engineering (all branches)
- meteorology
- operational research
- psychology
- quantity surveying
- teaching
- therapeutic radiography.

Further reading

Institute of Mathematics and its Applications: www.ima.org.uk

Maths Careers: www.mathscareers.org.uk

Media studies

Media is a worldwide industry, both reflecting and influencing society in most if not all aspects of life. Media can strongly influence the careers that young people aspire to, e.g. dramas such as *CSI* resulted in an increase in the numbers of people wanting to become forensic scientists! The growth of social media such as Facebook, Twitter and Snapchat have revolutionised mass communication, and indeed there are now occupations based on social media that did not exist until only a few years ago, e.g. social media marketing. By taking AS or A level, students develop an understanding of media products generally and how they are researched, produced, distributed and used. Formal qualifications do not guarantee a career in media, and for those who are seriously considering working in this sector, it is ESSENTIAL to start getting work experience relevant to the area sought. This might be writing for a school or college magazine or website, volunteering for hospital radio, working with any youth media organisations that operate in your area or helping with sound/lighting in school/college or amateur theatre productions. These sorts of activities can build a personal network of contacts who can be key to entry to media careers later.

What do you study?

Media studies involves the study and analysis of the media, i.e. television, radio, film, magazines and newspapers – what they are, how they work, the processes and technologies involved and their effect on audiences. It is both a practical and an academic subject in its coverage, but precise content will depend on the awarding body syllabus followed. Practical activities can include students assembling a project which could be a radio or television production, a newspaper or magazine article, which will involve working individually and with others. Students are also required to write an accompanying commentary on the project. Academic content includes the study of the languages and concepts of media: how words and images are used to represent ideas, the institutions of the media, production processes and technologies used, and the ways that audiences receive and consume information from the media. Good written English skills are required, and students must also be able to work both independently and in groups. Practical work can involve additional hours outside of usual college or sixth form times.

Why study media?

Media studies develops research and production skills which can be usefully employed in a variety of university courses. The subject also enhances students' skills of observation, critical analysis and self-reflection, plus their creativity and practical skills in audio-visual and written forms.

GCSE entry requirements

GCSE English language grade C/5 or above is the usual requirement. Media is useful but not essential.

How different from GCSE?

AS and A level build on topics covered at GCSE, e.g. media language, audiences and industries, but courses will be much more analytical, with longer written assignments, and much more reading is required.

How are the AS/A level assessed?

In England, AS level is assessed by one examination paper lasting between 2¼ and 2½ hours and a practical project to create a media product, with 70% of the marks coming from the examination and 30% from the project. A level is assessed by two examination papers, each lasting 2 hours, and a project involving the creation of a media product. The product for AS or A level could be a trailer for a TV programme, a TV advertisement, a news roundup, designing a new magazine or creating a website. The project may be specified or students may have a choice over the product they complete, so check on this with the school sixth form or college you intend going to. At A level, the project also contributes 30% to the overall marks and grade, with the remaining 70% assessed by examination papers. The WJEC (Welsh Joint Education Committee) Eduqas will be offering linear AS and A level media, with the same examination and project proportions contributing to final grades at AS and A level.

Combines well with

This depends on the area of media that students might want to work in. For study of media at university, subjects such as A level English (language or literature), government and politics, sociology, philosophy, drama and theatre studies, modern foreign languages or psychology combine well with media. Practical courses at universities involving use of visual media can benefit from A level art and design, and for technical areas of media, AS/A level mathematics, physics or design and technology (systems and control) can be an advantage.

Higher education suitability

Not a facilitating subject and students wanting to keep open the option of more competitive entry universities and/or subjects are advised to take two subjects from the list of facilitating A levels. Generally acceptable for higher education entry, but it is wise to check with universities on the acceptability of media studies if you are intending to study a non-media subject at more competitive entry institutions, or high entry requirement subjects.

Case study

Oliver Rossetti, from St Peter's Catholic School in Guildford, Surrey, took A level media studies. He said:

'I chose to study media studies, as my career goal was to become a film maker, and having supported my brother in his film production, I knew I had a keen eye for detail and loved the exciting atmosphere when on set. I enjoyed every minute of studying media studies as it pushed the boundaries of my knowledge when it came to film making and the theoretical side of the visual arts. It included making a short fictional film and a music video, both assessments requiring a written blog to be submitted and a reflective report. There were some long hours of editing, but having a professional, finished piece that you could call your own was a massive achievement and a life experience. There was a significant amount of team work, which developed a range of skills such as leadership and the ability to compromise when it came to developing ideas for films. In addition to the coursework, there were a couple of exams to assess your theoretical knowledge and ability to analyse clips from television and film. Media studies is not all about film and television making, it tests your ability to analyse and look for deeper meaning behind text; it is certainly not an easy subject, contrary to old beliefs. Before choosing, try writing a script, making a short film with a few friends and designing a storyboard to get a feel of how media studies may interest you. Also, start exploring different genres within film, television, literature and online/offline news; a good, well-rounded knowledge of different styles of telling a story to an audience is crucial.'

Media studies at university

Requirements to study media studies at degree level varies, as there are many media-based subjects at universities and colleges of art and design. For more design/visual-based degrees, A level art and design and even the Diploma in Foundation Studies (art and design) may be required, where a portfolio of work is needed. Some courses have a more sociological or humanities-based approach, and for these, essay-based subjects can be preferred, e.g. English (language or literature), history, government and politics or sociology. Technology-based courses, e.g. sound/broadcast engineering, can specify sciences as required, e.g. mathematics and/or physics or design and technology. It is a case of checking entry requirements carefully!

There are many courses at degree, Foundation degree and HNC/D (Higher National Certificate or Diploma) levels, and the content of such courses needs to be checked carefully. Some courses are more academic and analytical, others practical, some a combination. Some courses involve a work placement (sandwich course) in the industry, which can help to develop employability skills and improve job entry prospects. Examples of university courses include:

- broadcast media
- commercial video with multimedia
- creative film and moving image production
- digital media and marketing
- digital media and production
- film making
- interactive media and web analytics
- interactive media games art and animation
- media production (this can include options in radio or scriptwriting)
- practical journalism.

Media studies at university can be combined with other subjects, with English, politics or history being some of the most popular subject combinations.

Jobs with A level media studies

Some people begin their careers in film or television as 'runners' offering general assistance in the production of films or programmes. The website Creative Skillset (www.creativeskillset.org) advertises apprenticeships and has also established a network of screen academies recognised as centres of excellence for film education in the UK. Courses at these academies are offered at some colleges and universities and also include short technical courses. Some people start work in the industry in advertising and the distribution of films into cinema, or in marketing or administration roles. It is possible to join pre-entry journalism courses with A levels, although the great majority of professional journalists are graduates.

Graduate level jobs in media

Here are some occupational areas where the knowledge and skills gained through studying media at degree level can be useful:

- advertising account executive work
- broadcasting production research
- film/television camera operating
- journalism
- market research interviewing
- market research management
- marketing
- public relations
- television production/directing.

Further reading

BBC Careers: www.bbc.co.uk/careers/home

Creative and Cultural Skills – skills for craft, cultural heritage, design, literature, music, performing arts and visual arts: www.ccskills.org.uk

Creative Skillset – skills for the creative industries: www.creativeskillset.org

Modern foreign languages

The most common modern foreign languages (MFLs) at AS and A level are French, German and Spanish, but there are others including Arabic, Bengali, Chinese, Dutch, Gujarati, Italian, Japanese, Persian, Polish, Portuguese, Russian, Turkish and Urdu. *At the time of writing, it is not definite that all the above languages will be offered at AS or A level, owing to low take-up of some subjects or changes in awarding body policies.* The study of an MFL aims to develop high levels of skill in understanding, speaking and writing the language and a deeper knowledge of a particular country's culture and civilisation.

Modern foreign languages can help you gain access to top jobs in tourism, the media, the diplomatic service, translation and interpreting. Employers recognise linguists' skills beyond pure language ability, such as communication, organisation, cultural awareness and independence. In fact, graduates with knowledge of a foreign language are likely to earn more than graduates from other sectors.

What do you study?

Precise topics depend on the awarding body syllabus followed, but study of another language in all cases will involve four key areas.

- Speaking: this can be in pairs, in groups and/or onto a recording. This can include discussions, role play, debating and maintaining a conversation.
- Listening: this can include radio, television, plays, songs, poetry and interviews in the language.
- Reading: this can be novels (most commonly 20th century), newspapers, magazine articles and official documents.
- Writing: this can include creative pieces, essays, letters and summaries.

Typical AS and A level coverage includes many contemporary areas such as people and society, healthy living, leisure and sport, education, work and technology, all within an MFL context. It is essential to maintain detailed vocabulary and grammar notes, which will be used throughout the course. There can be frequent tests, comprehension and grammar exercises, translations and the preparation of texts for classroom study or oral presentation. The course is classroom based but often includes a study visit to the country in question, where students can be taught by native speakers, or an exchange visit which involves staying in that country for a short period of time. Lessons will usually be conducted in the language in question.

Why study MFLs?

Languages are among the most employable of subjects, given the international nature of work, trade and commerce in the modern world. Learning an MFL develops communication and problem-solving skills and also helps to improve social skills, confidence and overseas awareness. The knowledge of another language enhances career prospects, whatever is chosen to specialise in. Recent data from Oxford University shows that 93% of MFL university graduates go straight into employment or further study.

GCSE entry requirements

GCSE grade B/6 or higher in the language to be studied at AS/A level, and likewise in English language, are often required, unless you are a fluent speaker of the language in question.

How different from GCSE?

Where GCSE has been taken in a particular language, AS and A level require students to develop a much deeper understanding of how the language works than at GCSE, and much wider reading will be needed. A level languages build upon knowledge gained at GCSE, giving a sound understanding of using the language in a variety of contexts and situations at home, abroad, with friends or in the workplace.

How are the AS/A level assessed?

Assessment for French, German and Spanish is by examinations and spoken assessments. Precise format and structure of exams depend on the awarding body but there are similarities. AQA and OCR AS level comprise three papers or components; two are written (listening, reading, translation) and one is an oral test involving discussion of set topics in the language. Written exams last anything from 1¼ to 1¾ hours, and the oral 12 to 14 minutes. The Pearson Edexcel AS level has two written examination papers lasting 1 hour 40 minutes and 1¾ hours. A level for all the awarding bodies comprises three papers or components: two written (listening, reading, translation) and one oral assessment. Written papers last anything from 2 hours to 2 hours 40 minutes, the oral anything from 16 to 23, minutes, which includes a short amount of preparation time to read content cards. The A level oral includes discussion of a research project completed by the student. No dictionaries are permitted in ANY examinations or assessments for any of the awarding bodies. *For other languages at AS and A level, the government intends that these will be assessed along the same lines as French, German and Spanish.*

Combine well with

Another modern foreign or classical language will help to develop skills in and knowledge of the language, and vice versa. MFLs combine well with many other subjects, including sciences, computing and business. More common combinations with MFLs include English literature or language and history.

Recent A level results

French: Total students: 9,672 (Male: 3,093, Female: 6,579) Overall pass rate: 99.1%

A*	A	B	C	D	E	U
8.8	28.5	28.2	18.9	10.5	4.2	0.9

German: Total students: 3,842 (Male: 1,505, Female: 2,337) Overall pass rate: 99.5%

A*	A	B	C	D	E	U
9.6	30.0	28.4	19.0	9.3	3.2	0.5

Spanish: Total students: 8,460 (Male: 2,911, Female: 5,549) Overall pass rate: 99.2%

A*	A	B	C	D	E	U
8.4	26.0	31.3	20.4	10.0	3.1	0.8

Case study

Emily, from John Cleveland Sixth Form in Leicestershire, is taking A level French. She said:

'It's not just a case of memorising and reeling off vocabulary; it's about learning to appreciate the language and culture of France too. In fact in some respects the course is more like geography in that you have to understand the country, but this really helps as you become more able to communicate spontaneously. I love this subject and would encourage you to do it if you enjoyed GCSE. Ignore people who say that languages are useless; learning another language is so useful in the modern world where people work abroad. It's not just about learning the language you need to go on holiday!'

Higher education suitability

As a facilitating subject, an MFL is desirable for admission to more competitive entry universities and subjects generally. Universally accepted for entry to any degree subject, as long as other requirements are met. Particularly useful for business and engineering/science degrees, which may involve study or work abroad as part of the degree. Can also be used for entry to a wide range of other language degrees, as it demonstrates an aptitude for learning other languages.

MFLs at university

A core European language at A level is usually required for entry to a degree in the same language, e.g. A level French to study for a degree in French. For many other languages, e.g. Russian or Cantonese, universities will teach these to beginners, but will still expect a language A level as this demonstrates an aptitude for linguistics.

Degree courses can vary considerably. Some will be literature based, others will be more sociologically and language oriented. Language courses commonly include time studying abroad, e.g. for one year. It is often said that spending time abroad is the best way to learn a language and to experience the culture of the country. MFLs can be combined with many other languages at university, and also combine well with subjects such as business, economics, law, politics or engineering. There are European or other international degrees where a language will be incorporated within a subject such as engineering or law as opposed to being combined with it in the more traditional sense. Universities are increasingly giving undergraduates the opportunity of learning languages outside of their degree course to enhance their future employability. MFLs are available only as a degree, although there are HNC/D (Higher National Certificate or Diploma) and Foundation degree courses in travel and tourism subjects where a language option is available.

Jobs with A level in an MFL

Modern language A levels are an advantage (not requirement) for many occupational areas, especially those in the travel industry such as holiday representative or air cabin crew, but they are also useful for many types of work in the business and engineering worlds given the need for UK employers to trade overseas. Languages also help students to have a more open international outlook which is an advantage generally. There are international apprenticeships such as those offered in Germany through the IBA (International Business Academy). German language tuition is given as part of this 3 to 5 year apprenticeship but A level German would be an obvious advantage.

Graduate level jobs in MFLs

- Bilingual secretarial work
- Business and finance generally
- Journalism
- Professional linguistic work, e.g. translator or interpreter
- Recruitment consultancy

- Teaching
- Website/games translation
- Working in the travel and tourism industry.

Linguists are highly employable, as there is a need for graduates to have a global outlook and understanding of overseas cultures and societies. Anyone working in export sales and marketing is bound to talk on the telephone with or send emails to overseas contacts, and might also make visits to other countries. Language skills are also useful for freight forwarders, who offer services for importers and exporters, arranging things such as documentation and customs clearance.

Many organisations today are in partnership with foreign firms or have branches in other countries. This goes for the major banks, leading firms of lawyers and accountants, construction companies, insurance companies, landscape architects and many others. Language ability is useful for work in large advertising and marketing agencies, which are increasingly part of international groups.

Further reading

Chartered Institute of Linguists (CIOL): www.iol.org.uk

CILT: National Centre for Languages: www.cilt.org.uk

The Institute of Translation and Interpreting (ITI): www.iti.org.uk

Music

This is a subject where an active interest and ability are essential for success, rather than just a liking for listening to music. At AS and A level students cover performance, musical theory, composition and history of music, with some awarding body specifications covering the study of world music, jazz, folk, film and television music and classical music in Western cultures. Music is a form of communication and therefore it is like learning another language where structure and form need to be learned. A considerable amount of listening and practice is required if a good grade is to be achieved, and students must be prepared to listen to a broad range of musical styles apart from their own preferences.

What do you study?

The specifications of the awarding bodies are very similar, although there can be different emphases between them. Typically, courses will cover the following.

- Listening: students learn how to listen and analyse music through dictation, and description of music samples.
- Composing: the techniques of musical composition are learned through imitating particular styles, e.g. from early Romantic keyboard accompaniment and choral harmonisation through to modern genres including folk, pop, hip hop and dance. Composing also involves musical arrangement for a particular instrument or group of instruments which is sent for assessment in recorded form.
- Performing: this involves preparation of a recital, the duration depending on the awarding body specification followed.
- The history of music: this can include music for film and television, jazz, popular music, orchestral music in the 18th and 19th centuries and popular instrumental music from 1900 to the present day.
- Analysis and appreciation of music: musical structures and techniques, including harmony, melody, tonality, texture, rhythm, sonata and counterpoint.

Study of classical music can be compulsory and will include genres such as Baroque (Purcell, Vivaldi, Bach) or Mozart operas, and the Romantic composers such as Chopin, Brahms and Grieg.

Lessons will include listening to music and group discussions and analyses of pieces. Students need to be prepared to listen to a wide range of musical types so as to develop their ability to listen effectively. Also, attendance at live events will enhance these skills and demonstrate an active interest in the subject, which will be needed for university entry to music-based courses. Some sixth forms or colleges may require students to have additional instrument lessons outside of their AS/A level course. Students work together in the composition and performance of pieces and so they must be prepared to listen to each other and compromise where needed.

GCSE entry requirements

GCSE music is not always essential, but where it has been taken, sixth forms and colleges will often require a grade B/6. Alternatively, if the student has a proven talent for the subject, e.g. ability to play a particular instrument or instruments (or vocal ability), this can be an acceptable alternative. A certain standard of proficiency in the Associated Board of the Royal Schools of Music examinations (often referred to as 'grades') for an instrument or singing will be needed, e.g. grade 3 minimum in theory and performance where GCSE music has not been taken. I have heard an A level music teacher say that grade 5 music theory is actually a better grounding for A level music than GCSE.

How different from GCSE?

AS and A level build on the skills developed at GCSE, but students develop aural, theoretical and analytical skills, enabling them to explore a significant 'set work' and specialist area of study. Students will also need to listen to a variety of music genres and practise their performance skills much more than at GCSE.

How are the AS/A level assessed?

The timings of examination papers and performance and composition assessments vary according to the awarding body specification. AS level assessment is similar across the awarding bodies, comprising three components: typically an examination paper and/or an aural perception test lasting from 1 to 2 hours and covering listening, analysis and an essay or shorter answer format questions, a performance piece (solo or as part of an ensemble – voice or instrument) lasting at least 6 to 8 minutes which is recorded (audio-visual) and posted or uploaded to the awarding body, and a composition lasting from 3 to 4½ minutes, which again is sent to the awarding body. There are set dates (usually between March and May) when performance and composition pieces must be submitted to the awarding bodies. In some cases a visiting examiner will observe performances by students.

A level assessment is essentially the same but performance and composition pieces are generally longer, e.g. a minimum of 8 to 12 minutes of performance music, and 5 to 9 minutes for the compositions. The written examinations range in duration from 1¼ to 2½ hours. Check with the college or sixth form you intend going to about the music briefs required and timings. A commentary on the composition written may also be required.

Combines well with

Languages are especially useful if you are considering a professional singing career, e.g. classical opera is often sung in Italian, German or Spanish. Mathematics, physics and computing are very useful (and in some cases necessary) for electronic or technology-based music courses, including sound engineering.

Case study

Sophia, from Bryanston School in Dorset, said about A level music:

'I chose this subject because I love playing saxophone, performing, and I have been surrounded by music from a young age. I also chose music because I wanted to expand my knowledge and understanding and then apply this to my interpretation of pieces. The topics and pieces are studied in much more depth than at GCSE. For example, we studied part of Haydn's Symphony No. 104 in D major in the first year, and are currently studying the whole of Elgar's Symphony in A flat major. For GCSE, I studied 12 pieces in what seems like very little detail by comparison; however, it definitely contributed to my understanding of what we study at A level. In Elgar's Symphony, we look in detail at the harmonic, melodic, structural features and so on, together with the effect that it may have on the listener. It is hard work. There are effectively five sub-sections of music that we learn about; aural, composition, performance, origins of jazz and Elgar's Symphony – each is difficult to master. I believe that anyone would benefit from learning these skills because the analytical process and comprehension can be applied to any subject. In my opinion it covers more than an A level because there are so many different skills, which do relate to other subjects.

'Even listening to Radio 3 frequently, even without the background knowledge, is a good idea because it is an example of how people beyond A level discuss and talk about music and composers' styles. For the performance part of the subject, one needs to play an instrument. I believe that the standard required for final A level performance recordings is grade 8 in order to obtain a top grade overall. Before taking the exam I would assume that the student already plays an instrument, but if not it is possible to take A level without being at this standard. If someone has not very much background knowledge, I would suggest that they dedicate enough time to listening to classical music (including Baroque, Classical and Romantic periods) and learn an instrument or to sing. The A level course is now taken after two years, so being grade 8 standard in the first year is not required, but of course it helps.

'Music is a very important subject. It is important for creating unity among people. People play their instruments because they love playing music. For me I find that it transports me to an unknown place and for lots of people to feel the same way simultaneously is something that I think the world could do with more of. Although this seems rather far-fetched, understanding the concepts of what one studies at A level, even if the desired grade is not obtained, contributes to achieving this. Music is a subject that everyone can relate to and it has a positive effect on anyone.'

Recent A level results

Total students: 6,293 **(Male: 3,584, Female: 2,709)** **Overall pass rate: 98.6%**

A*	A	B	C	D	E	U
4.0	14.7	25.9	27.7	18.9	7.4	1.4

Higher education suitability

Not a facilitating subject, but acceptable as an AS/A level subject for entry to most if not all university courses, as long as other requirements are met. Students aiming to enter competitive entry universities/degrees are advised to take at least two facilitating subjects.

Music at university

A level music will usually be required for entry to music degree courses at university. In many cases an Associated Board of the Royal Schools of Music grade 8 in a musical instrument or voice will also be required, and in some instances a grade 5 to 6 in a second instrument may be needed where the degree is performance based. Degree courses with a performance focus will require an audition and interview, and possibly some other form of assessment, e.g. a sight-reading or listening test.

Degrees in music are most commonly awarded as a BMus (Bachelor of Music) or BA. The BMus degree will focus more on performance, composition or history of music, whereas the BA is broader in scope. The first two years of a degree will build on skills and knowledge gained from A level study, with the third year allowing for more specialisation. Specialisms can include study of particular periods of music, stringed instruments, piano or more modern topics including jazz, popular or rock music, or use of computers in composition. Some courses offer the opportunity to study abroad at an overseas university or conservatoire. In the UK there are nine conservatoires, which offer more performance-based degree courses:

- Birmingham Conservatoire
- Guildhall School of Music and Drama
- Leeds College of Music
- The Royal Academy of Music
- The Royal College of Music
- The Royal Conservatoire of Scotland
- The Royal Northern College of Music
- The Royal Welsh College of Music and Drama
- Trinity Laban Conservatoire of Music and Dance.

The Guildhall School of Music and Drama recruits directly and does not use UCAS for applications.

Music can be studied as a single subject or in combination with others, with subjects such as performing arts or visual arts being among the more popular.

However, there are many subject combinations possible. There is a link between musical ability and mathematical aptitude.

Aside from degrees, there are also Foundation degrees in subjects such as music performance, applied music practice, community music, music technology, song writing and music composition for film and media. There are HNC/D (Higher National Certificate or Diploma) courses in subjects such as music performance, music business, music technology and sound engineering. Entry requirements for these are generally lower than for a degree, with a minimum of one A level pass grade and another subject studied but not necessarily passed at A level. Subjects can be specified, e.g. mathematics or physics for sound engineering, music for music performance courses. Entry requirements can be higher than the above, so check university and college sites carefully.

Jobs with A level music

In the music industry, some people with A level start in roles as assistants in areas such as broadcasting, recording or music journalism and work their way up. The skills learned from A level music, especially the discipline of practice and experience of working with others on compositions, can be readily transferred to a wide range of jobs and apprenticeships where subjects are not specified.

Graduate level jobs in music

- Composing, e.g. for film, computer games or song writing
- Music business management
- Music journalism
- Music technology/musical instrument technology
- Music therapy
- Professional musician
- Teaching
- Working in the media industry.

Further reading

BPI: British Recorded Music Industry: www.bpi.co.uk

Creative and Cultural Skills – skills for craft, cultural heritage, design, literature, music, performing arts and visual arts: www.ccskills.org.uk

Incorporated Society of Musicians (ISM): www.ism.org

Music Education Council (MEC): www.mec.org.uk

Music technology

This subject involves the study of how music is composed and recorded, especially the use of computer technology. On the practical side, music technology involves the recording of live music, use of digital recording techniques, composition using computer sequencers and creating a performance from a music score on a computer. On the theoretical side, it includes listening to music from all the ages, but particularly film and popular music, using music theory and technology language to analyse popular music, and also covers the study of the history of music technology.

What do you study?

Topics covered will include the following.

- Sequencing, recording and producing: this involves learning the skills needed to produce music performances in a range of styles using sequencing software and multi-track recording equipment.
- Music composition using technology to create compositions to a brief set by the awarding body.
- Arranging and improvisation: this involves taking a melody or short sequence of notes to develop it into a full arrangement recorded on a CD or as a score.
- Listening to and analysing the development of popular music from the early 20th century to the present day; a range of genres will be covered which can include rock, hip hop, rap, reggae, heavy metal, soul, punk, new wave and club dance.

Music technology is a practical subject and students will spend a lot of time creating recordings and sequencing using a range of technology. Students are advised to listen to a broad range of music beyond what is covered in lessons so as to recognise the structure and technology used in arrangements.

Why study music technology?

Music technology is used in all types of music, ranging from classical to the most modern genres. The subject enables students to arrange and compose music to a high standard and also to understand the technologies used. This will enhance prospects for employment in many roles in the music industry, as shown below.

GCSE entry requirements

GCSE music at grade C/5 or above may be required, unless students have relevant experience. GCSE ICT is useful, but by no means essential, although good computer skills are necessary. The ability to play an instrument is usually required, up to grades 4 to 6 of the Associated Board of the Royal Schools of Music, and grade 3 or above in music theory. Check with individual institutions on their requirements, as they can vary.

How are the AS/A level assessed?

At the time of writing Pearson Edexcel is the only awarding body to offer music technology as an AS or A level qualification. Two non-examination activities in which students compose and produce two sets of material from briefs set by Pearson, using instruments and technology specified, account for 40% of the AS level assessment. The produced pieces are 2 to 2½ minutes long.

The other 60% of the AS level is assessed by two examinations which last 1¼ and 1¾ hours and comprise compulsory questions only. Questions are a mix of practical and theory, including use of MIDI and audio materials on one examination paper, and listening and analysing.

The structure of the A level assessment is similar and comprises two non-examination activities where students produce pieces lasting 3 to 3½ and 3 minutes' duration. This accounts for 40% of the A level assessment. There are two examination papers lasting 1½ and 2¼ hours which account for 60% of the A level grade.

Combines well with

Music, mathematics, physics, electronics and computing all fit well with music technology; see below for entry requirements to study this subject at university.

Higher education suitability

Not a facilitating subject, although generally acceptable for entry to higher education, as long as other requirements are met.

Music technology at university

Requirements to study music technology at degree level depends on the course in question, as content can vary. Courses with a sound engineering emphasis are likely to require A levels in mathematics and physics, or possibly electronics or computing. Courses with a performance bias will likely require A level music and may require an audition.

Case study

Daniel Taylor, from Greenhead College, took A level music technology. He said:

'It looked like an interesting subject that would complement my music A level, giving a much broader and in-depth perspective of music, including the technical and production aspects of modern music. Most lessons involve working on computers and getting on with the creative processes. You spend a lot of time with headphones on. To begin with, you just get used to the programs and how to do certain things with them. Then it's a very individual subject. Everyone's projects end up different and there's such an array of creative ideas that circulate the room. There are a few lessons a week in which we study musical periods, currently being Rock and Roll and Rap and Hip Hop. These go very in-depth with recording processes, microphones and technology used and instrumentation. Don't think that it's an easy subject; it takes a very long time to perfect your work. It's a good subject to take if you have an interest in music but don't necessarily play an instrument or don't have any classical music background. It's also very rewarding when finishing coursework and creating something unique and professional.'

Degree titles can include: creative music technology, creative sound production, music technology, sound technology, sound engineering or music and sound. Some degree courses will be sound engineering based, while others will be more performance oriented. Degrees awarded can be BMus (Bachelor of Music), BA (Bachelor of Arts), BEng (Bachelor of Engineering) or BSc (Bachelor of Science). BEng degrees are for those wishing to become sound engineers or designers of electronic instruments and studio equipment. ***It is important to check that courses are accredited by APRS – the Association of Professional Recording Services – as this will be needed if you are seeking employment in the sound and recording industry after graduation.***

Music technology can be combined with other subjects at university, with the more popular including performing arts, media, broadcasting and music performance. Music technology can also be combined with sciences, computing or management subjects. Content of courses can vary considerably and students are advised to check this carefully with individual institutions and not to choose courses by subject title alone.

Aside from degree courses, there are also Foundation degree and HNC/D (Higher National Certificate or Diploma) courses in a wide range of music technology-based subjects, including creative sound technology, music technology, sound engineering, music production, popular music production and performance and DJ and electronic music.

Jobs with A level music technology

As with film and media A levels and their respective industries, employment in the sound and recording industry can be as a 'runner' or assistant in places such as radio stations, live concerts or theatres. There are apprenticeships in sound and music technology, but availability in particular areas of the country will vary.

Graduate level jobs in music technology

Possible employment will depend on the content of the qualification completed. Examples include working in audio production, radio, TV or internet broadcasting, live sound engineering, e.g. concerts, theatre, teaching in schools, colleges or university (postgraduate teacher training will be required), music technology journalism, software design, sound design, studio engineering, music management and promotion. Contracts can be on a short-term basis, and so self-employment is very likely. Aside from the above, the computer and engineering skills learned from some of the degree courses can be used to enter the information technology and engineering sectors, as well as arts administration and events management.

Further reading

Creative and Cultural Choices: www.creative-choices.co.uk

Creative and Cultural Skills: www.ccskills.org.uk

Creative Skillset: www.creativeskillset.org

Joint Audio Media Education Support (JAMES): www.jamesonline.org.uk

Philosophy

The word 'philosophy' originates from the ancient Greek word meaning 'love of wisdom'. The ancient Greeks founded philosophy, and the questions they pondered are still examined by modern philosophers to this day. The core issue of philosophy is whether or not we can rationally justify our beliefs and opinions, especially in the areas of reality (metaphysics), knowledge (epistemology), moral judgement (ethics) and language (semantics). Questions that philosophy asks include the following.

- Is there anything we can know with certainty?
- What is truth?
- What is justice?
- How is the human mind related to the body?
- Are there any absolute moral values?
- Does God exist?

Philosophy does not answer questions like this but teaches students how to approach and analyse them. It is a subject that will appeal to 'thinkers' who enjoy grappling with abstract ideas and theories; it is unlikely to suit those who have a more practical outlook.

What do you study?

AS level subject matter covers the following.

- Epistemology: do we know anything for certain? Is there any difference between knowledge and belief?
- Moral philosophy: are there moral truths and, if so, what are their nature?

A level subject matter covers the following.

- Epistemology.
- Moral philosophy.
- Metaphysics of God: the study of existence; everything that exists and the nature of existence.
- Metaphysics of mind: can your mind exist independently, or is it dependent on something else in order to exist? In particular, is your mind dependent on your body, perhaps especially your brain, in order to exist at all?

Aside from a considerable amount of reading, philosophy requires students to engage in class discussions and group presentations. You are likely to be challenged on your viewpoints and understanding of some difficult ideas. Reading can be demanding; initially at least as you need to be able to grasp how philosophical arguments are presented. Philosophical terminology needs to be understood and applied, e.g. assertion/claim, proposition, antecedent/consequent, analytic/synthetic, a priori/a posteriori, necessary/contingent, consistent/inconsistent, objective/subjective, tautology, dilemma, paradox, prove/proof, true/false and justification. Written work in the form of essays will be required. Set texts encountered can include works by famous philosophers such as Descartes, Sartre, Nietzsche, Berkeley, Kant, Mill, Gettier, Hume, Plato, Russell and Zagzebski.

Why study philosophy?

Philosophy develops the ability to reason, analyse and to argue both logically and confidently, which are skills that can be usefully employed in a wide range of university subjects and occupations, with notable examples including law, politics and journalism. This subject can reinforce skills learned from related subjects such as law, English, history, psychology, mathematics and religious studies, and indeed the reverse is also true.

GCSE entry requirements

GCSE grade C/5 or above in English language is usually required, as philosophy requires the ability to write well-structured essays and understand unusual vocabulary as shown above. Mathematics is a subject based on logic and reason, and so those with an aptitude for mathematics may benefit from studying philosophy, although a high grade at GCSE is not generally required.

How different from GCSE?

There is no GCSE in philosophy, although OCR offers GCSE religious studies, which emphasises philosophy and ethics. As with other subjects, you need a lot of intellectual curiosity and a readiness to listen to others' viewpoints in order to benefit from the study of philosophy at A level. Essays will be longer and need to demonstrate a higher level of understanding than those written for GCSE religious studies, and much wider reading will be required.

How are the AS/A level assessed?

At the time of writing, the new AS and A level specifications are in draft format so the information below is yet to be finalised. AQA is the only awarding body for AS and A level philosophy. The AS level is assessed by one examination paper lasting 3 hours and comprising two sections, each containing five questions.

The A level is assessed by two examination papers, each lasting 3 hours, and again each comprising two sections with five questions in each.

Combines well with

Any subjects which develop the ability to write good essays and also present logical arguments, e.g. English literature or language, history, government and politics, religious studies or psychology. Mathematics A level develops logical thinking skills, which fits with philosophy.

Higher education suitability

Not a facilitating subject, but acceptable for entry to university generally, as long as other requirements are met. An essay-based subject, making it a good preparation for any such courses at university.

Case study

Monty, from Bryanston School, Dorset, said about philosophy:

'The subject is what I hoped it would be, with plenty of opportunities to ask questions and debate issues. I don't go to a philosophy lesson thinking, "oh no this is going to be so boring"; instead, I look forward to sitting around as a group and discussing the subject. One of the best skills that I have learned from this topic, which I think is an incredibly useful skill for today's "post-truth" society, is critical evaluation: you examine an argument, say, for the existence of God, and then you try to break down whether the argument stacks up, its strengths and weaknesses, looking at key scholars who agree and disagree. I have found this skill to be incredibly useful in everyday life, helping me not to take everything at face value but actually think about what I am being told, rather than blindly accepting it. Another joy of philosophy is the fact that with a lot of the issues discussed there is no right answer. What this means is that you can formulate your personal opinion, which you can then debate with others. Overall the subject is very enjoyable to study and strikes a good balance between challenge and fun. Philosophy is an essay-based subject so be prepared for that! But my best advice is, if you like to question things, are inquisitive and enjoy a good discussion, don't hesitate to study philosophy!'

Philosophy at university

A level philosophy is not generally required to study the subject at university, although having taken it will demonstrate an interest and enhance a university application, as well as provide an insight into philosophy. Mathematics can be a preferred subject, owing to its logical basis.

Content of degree courses can vary considerably. Some will focus on contemporary issues connected to philosophy, e.g. in education, religion or politics, while others will involve study of great philosophers such as Plato and Aristotle. Courses will usually introduce students to the main types of philosophical arguments, and in some cases the first year will cover humanities more widely, with philosophy being just one of the subjects covered. Degree courses will commonly have optional topics to choose from, including the philosophy and history of science, feminist philosophy (this means the position of women in society), aesthetics (how we judge art and beauty), European philosophy, or study of particular philosophers, e.g. Nietzsche, Hegel or Wittgenstein. Philosophy can be combined with other subjects at university, e.g. with politics, psychology, history, economics, religious studies, modern languages or sciences. There are no Foundation degree or HNC/D (Higher National Certificate or Diploma) courses in philosophy, although subjects such as law/legal studies at this level involve logical argument.

Jobs with A level philosophy

There are no jobs in philosophy at this level but, as with other subjects, the skills developed through studying it at A level can be usefully employed. Jobs which require the ability to think logically and present a well-reasoned argument can benefit from the study of philosophy, e.g. sales, marketing, administration or management generally.

Graduate level jobs in philosophy

Aside from university lecturers who are involved with research as well as teaching, there are few opportunities to work directly in philosophy. Teaching in schools and colleges is possible, but in the case of schools, graduates would need to be able to offer a national curriculum subject to teach, e.g. religious studies or history. As with holders of A level philosophy, the skills developed can be used in sales, marketing, administrative or management roles in particular. In fact, it is surprising just how many career paths a philosophy degree can help with. Studying philosophy can make a significant contribution to any job that requires an ability to think well, that is, clearly. Business, including the City firms, banks, management consultancies and chartered accountants are enthusiastic about people who have studied philosophy, because they know how to think clearly. Philosophy students also go into law, politics and the civil service. Journalism is another potential career path, since you have to be able to write well and present ideas logically and clearly.

Further reading

www.alevelphilosophy.co.uk

The Royal Institute of Philosophy: www.royalinstitutephilosophy.org

Photography

Photography is studied as a branch of art and design. There is an emphasis on creative expression and enquiry, which means the production, selection and manipulation of images to produce different meanings. A significant amount of the course will involve practical projects enabling students to build a comprehensive portfolio of their work, which they will need if they intend going on to higher education courses in creative media subjects.

What do you study?

Students learn how to use cameras effectively, both digital and film based. They also learn how to use a darkroom, work in a studio environment and use digital media software. Aside from these practical skills, students develop a better understanding of images, they learn to analyse critically the work of others and also study the history of photography. Precise content of the course depends on the awarding body syllabus covered, but typically will include:

- animation
- commercial photography
- documentary photography
- editorial photography
- experimental imagery
- landscape photography
- moving image, i.e. film making
- photographic installation
- portraiture
- still life photography
- the photographic process.

Within the above, students learn how to use photographic equipment, also the detailed techniques required to develop photographs, how colour photography differs from black and white, how to manipulate light effectively, how to represent people, inanimate objects and the natural environment through photography and how to interpret and work to a given brief.

Photography is by definition a practical subject, and so students must be prepared to go out to varying types of location to capture images, e.g. landscapes, city images, images taken outdoors at night. Students must also be prepared to do extra work outside of lesson times and in most cases will need to have their own equipment such as a digital SLR (single lens reflex) camera, film SLR, tripod and memory stick, although colleges and sixth forms will usually have equipment that can be loaned to students. There are also likely to be visits to galleries and exhibitions. There will be class-based discussions, and you must be prepared to write essays!

Why study photography?

As with art and design, photography develops the ability to present information creatively and effectively. In addition, students learn how to critically analyse pieces of work. The observational and evaluative skills they learn are useful for areas such as advertising, marketing, public relations or working in TV and other media; all require the ability to communicate effectively in a visual format. Some university graduates move into areas such as arts administration, e.g. the running of art galleries and exhibitions. The creative industries sector is one of the fastest growing in the UK at this time, and the modern world of work is witnessing a convergence of arts and sciences, where creative skills are needed alongside the ability to solve problems and work with complex situations.

GCSE entry requirements

GCSE photography is useful but not a general requirement to take AS or A level in the subject. Some colleges or school sixth forms may prefer or even require a design or art-based subject at GCSE; it is a case of checking individual institutions' entry criteria.

How different from GCSE?

AS and A level involve a lot more research and development of ideas than at GCSE, and students will need to be prepared to commit a lot more time to the subject. Written assignments will be longer and need to demonstrate a greater depth of understanding when analysing the work of others.

How are the AS/A level assessed?

The format and content of AS and A level photography is broadly similar across all the awarding bodies. Typically the subject is assessed by two components: a portfolio/personal investigation of photography, and an externally assessed assignment in which students have an extended period of time to prepare, and between 10 and 15 hours of supervised time to produce the work required. The portfolio generally accounts for 60% and the assignment for 40% of the overall AS level and A level grades (50%:50% in the case of Pearson Edexcel). A written narrative of between 1,000 and 3,000 words is also required to support the work presented, the precise length depending on the awarding body requirements.

Combines well with

Art and design will help students to build a strong portfolio, but be aware that some universities may consider that there is too much overlap between the subjects and accept only one of them in the A level offer they make. Academic subjects such as English or history develop the ability to write effectively, which would be useful for photography, and also media studies where moving images are explored as a means of communication. A modern foreign language will enhance your prospects generally. If you intend going into more technical fields of photography, e.g. medical or forensic photography, one or more sciences at A level would be a good choice.

Higher education suitability

Not a facilitating subject, but acceptable for entry to a wide range of university courses, as long as specific requirements are met. Students seeking entry to more competitive subjects or universities generally are advised to include two facilitating subjects in their A level choices.

 **Case study**

Daisy Stimpson, from Stroud High School, took A level photography. She said:

> *'I have an interest in art and design as well as being dyslexic. This course suited me as it is coursework based and does not rely on completing a written exam at the end. It allowed me to improve on a skill I was passionate about as a hobby and helped me to build a portfolio for university applications. This subject was one of my favourites at A Level. It allowed me freedom and to choose what aspects of the subject I wanted to explore. I enjoyed the support I received on the course; because the classes were smaller there was more focus on our work from the teachers. I would say that students shouldn't choose it if they think it's just a filler or 'easy' subject. It's a lot of work, and you have to be on top of your work all year, you can't leave things to the last minute. I'd also say that there are lots of people who think it is 'not a real subject'; don't listen to them! If you think photography is for you, go for it. If you work hard and do well, then it's not a waste of an option, and there are loads of jobs (and uni courses) it can lead to. Even though I didn't do any creative GCSEs I did both art and photography at A Level, and am currently doing a degree in graphic design. It goes to show that even if you didn't make the right choice at GCSE it's not the end of the world.'*

Photography at university

Lens-based media courses at university are likely to require a good portfolio of work to show at interview, and therefore completion of a Diploma in Foundation Studies in art and design is recommended after A levels.

Photography can be studied as a single subject at university or in combination with others. There are different course titles, including photographic art, photographic practice, contemporary lens media and contemporary photography. It is important to check the content of university courses carefully to ensure that they will meet your interests, and not to rely on course titles alone. Many university courses will allow students to specialise in the second or third year; this might be in medical, landscape, portraiture, industrial, marine, fashion, fine art, cinema photography or photojournalism. Other subjects that students more commonly take alongside photography include video, fashion, public relations or digital imaging.

Apart from degree courses, there are also Foundation degree and HNC/D (Higher National Certificate or Diploma) courses, e.g. digital photography, professional photography, photo imaging or applied photography. Entry requirements for these are generally lower than for a degree; check with individual universities to ascertain that there is an option to top up the HND or Foundation degree to a full degree qualification.

Jobs with A level photography

Some people enter this work through being an assistant to a professional photographer, learning the techniques of photography. Others start their careers by working in photographic equipment shops or professional development and printing laboratories. Some will start by working for local newspapers as trainee press photographers. Aside from photography-based occupations, people with A level photography learn skills that can be usefully employed in other areas of work, e.g. visual merchandising in shops, advertising, marketing or public relations.

Graduate level jobs in photography

Photographers work in a wide range of settings, including journalism, product photography, e.g. food for cookery magazines or books, fashion/clothing photography, police work (photographing scenes of crime), travel photography, e.g. for holiday brochures, medical photography, wildlife photography, as well as photography for weddings and other important social gatherings. Around half of all photographers are self-employed and so a good head for business is required in many cases. Building a strong portfolio of work is vital as this will be the basis for finding work opportunities by showing your skills. The skills learned from studying photography can be readily used in other areas of work where the visual image is important, e.g. in advertising, visual merchandising in shops, graphic design and publishing. Teaching is another possibility, which might be in schools, colleges or universities. Further training will be required to attain the professional recognition required for teaching.

Further reading

British Journal of Photography: www.bjp-online.com

The Royal Photographic Society: www.rps.org

Physical education

Physical activity, or perhaps more accurately *lack of physical activity*, is often in the news, with frequent reporting of sedentary lifestyles, obesity, especially among children, and poor health as being a drain on an already overstretched health service. This, coupled with recent successes such as the 2012 London and 2016 Rio Olympics and Paralympics has given a new impetus for people to lead more active lifestyles and to participate more in sport. This has led to an increase in opportunities to work in the sport and fitness sector in a range of roles. The entry level for employment in this area ranges from jobs that require no academic qualifications, to those that need a degree or postgraduate qualification. Some of the occupations require sports coaching, leadership or supervisory awards. The majority who study physical education do so because it builds upon previous sporting experiences and allows students to develop their knowledge and understanding of specific roles and responsibilities they prefer, therefore encouraging excellence in their chosen activity.

What do you study?

AS and A level physical education are mostly classroom-based courses covering theoretical content. This includes the following.

- Anatomy, which is the physical structure of the body and how the body responds to physical activity.
- Physiology, which is the functioning of the body.
- Psychology, which is the study of behaviour and its effects on performance.
- Application of anatomical and physiological knowledge to improve sport performance: this includes study of aerobics, anaerobics, muscles, preparation and training, mechanics of movement, energy sources and sports injuries.
- Critical analysis to improve sports performance: this can involve students demonstrating how they have improved performance in particular sports through selecting, applying and developing certain skills.
- Investigation into current issues in physical education.

Some specifications enable students to demonstrate practical skills from a choice of activities, e.g. team games/gymnastics/athletics/outdoor adventure sports or water sports, including swimming. Students are expected to participate in practical sports and to be assessed on their performance. Students will take on the role of either performer or coach in one physical activity and develop their skills, recording their achievements and developments within this area. They will then analyse their performances throughout the course in assignments which will inform them of the progress they have made.

Why study physical education?

A level physical education supports a wide range of future study and careers, such as sport professional, working in leisure and fitness centres, physiotherapy, journalism, coaching, nutrition or teaching. Many students go on to university to study courses in sport science, sports engineering, sports management, exercise science, physical education, physiotherapy or sports nutrition.

GCSE entry requirements

GCSE physical education is not a general requirement, although having taken it will give a useful insight into the subject. Grade C/5 or above in science can sometimes be required.

How different from GCSE?

AS and A level build on topics covered in GCSE physical education theory, but greater depth of understanding is required, and also more analysis of one's own and others' performance in the practical aspects covered. There is a lot of individual study, mostly reading around the subject to strengthen your knowledge. This is ESSENTIAL if higher grades are to be achieved. The topics covered can be different from GCSE, so make sure that you know what is on offer at the college or sixth form you intend going to.

How are the AS/A level assessed?

Assessment is broadly similar across the awarding bodies. Examinations for AS level range from 1 hour's to 2 hours' duration and comprise one or more papers, depending on the awarding body. Questions are a mix of multi-choice, short answer and extended response in format. The grade is made up of 70% from examinations and 30% from a sport performance or coaching activity set by the college or sixth form. This also includes a written analysis of the activity by the student. A level is assessed 70% by examinations, comprising from one to three papers lasting from 1 hour to 2½ hours, and 30% by a performance or coaching activity.

Combines well with

Biology, psychology, sociology. Business studies or economics can be useful if you are intending to go into leisure and recreation management.

Recent A level results

Total students: 11,627 **(Male: 7,100, Female: 4,527)** **Overall pass rate: 97.7%**

A*	A	B	C	D	E	U
3.3	12.5	23.8	25.6	20.6	11.9	2.3

Case study

Zaneta, from Herefordshire, is now a physical education (PE) teacher. She said:

'I chose my three subjects because of my interest in them. I knew I could do well in art and PE and that having an A level in maths would be very useful in the future. At the point of choosing my A levels I wasn't sure what I was going to do as a career, but I knew that improving and developing my current strengths was a good way to start. Sport was really enjoyable, as the lessons were proactive, innovative and inclusive. Teachers offered a lot of good support too. There was much more organisation and planning involved than at GCSE to finish assignments. As a PE teacher, I have experienced teaching A level and I've seen how pupils can struggle with the content of the course if they don't keep up with learning and understanding topics. You need to come to PE with full commitment, passion for the subject and a really good knowledge base gained from GCSE. A lot of people see PE as an easy subject and they don't realise how much demanding theory is involved.'

Higher education suitability

Not a facilitating subject, but acceptable generally for university entry, as long as other requirements are met. Students aiming to go to more competitive entry universities and/or to study subjects apart from sport are advised to take two facilitating subjects at A level.

Sport at university

A science at A level, especially biology or chemistry, is advised if you are aiming to study sport science or physical education at university. Some will accept A level psychology or physical education as an alternative to one of the natural sciences. Taking an active part in sport outside of school or college will enhance your university application, and there are many opportunities to study abroad, especially in the USA, if students have particular talents in sport. Maintaining an active and healthy lifestyle, with a good diet and abstinence from alcohol, drug use and smoking will be essential!

There are MANY courses with sport titles at universities. These include:

- community sport development
- equine sports coaching
- health and personal training
- outdoor adventure management
- physical education and coaching
- sport and exercise science
- sport and leisure management
- sport business
- sport coaching
- sport conditioning, rehabilitation and massage/therapy
- sport development
- sport journalism
- sport management
- sport science
- sports studies
- surf science and technology.

Some courses, e.g. coaching, have specialisms in particular sports, e.g. rugby, golf or football. Courses are available at degree, Foundation degree and HNC/D (Higher National Certificate or Diploma) levels. It is important to check the CONTENT of courses carefully and not to rely on titles alone, and also the facilities available and the links which the universities have with the sports industry. Sport can also be combined with other subjects at university, e.g. human biology, business, languages or management, but there are many other possibilities.

Jobs with A level physical education

Examples include leisure centre assistant, lifeguard in a swimming pool, coach/instructor, personal trainer, outdoor pursuits instructor, working in sport equipment and clothing retail, and working with pupils in schools to take up more active interests and exercise. Note that A levels are not a requirement for entry to these occupations, although they would enhance prospects for getting into management levels later. People often start through apprenticeships for these sorts of occupations. Other types of work are also open to people with A levels generally, including business administration, customer service, retail and healthcare.

Graduate level jobs in sport

These include:

- jobs in sport medicine
- lecturer in further and higher education
- physical education teacher
- sport and leisure centre manager
- sports development officer
- sports scientist
- sports therapist.

Aside from the above, the skills developed from studying sport can be used for entry into other occupations, e.g. management generally, finance, youth and community work, social work, journalism, the emergency and armed services.

Further reading

Association for Physical Education (AfPE): www.afpe.org.uk

Skills Active: www.skillsactive.com

Sport England: www.sportengland.org

Physics

The main goal of physics is to understand how the universe behaves. It is one of the oldest academic disciplines, perhaps the oldest, through its inclusion of astronomy. Over nearly 2,000 years physics was a part of natural philosophy along with chemistry, biology and certain branches of mathematics, but during the scientific revolution in the 17th century the natural sciences emerged as unique research subjects in their own right. Physics intersects with many interdisciplinary areas of research, such as biophysics and quantum chemistry, and the boundaries of physics are not rigidly defined. New ideas in physics often explain the fundamental mechanisms of other sciences, while opening new avenues of research in areas such as mathematics and philosophy.

What do you study?

The precise content depends on the awarding body syllabus followed, but typically, content will include the following.

- The properties of matter, including liquids, solids and gases, mechanical, thermal and electrical properties in molecular terms.
- The properties of materials, including density and Young's modulus.
- Oscillations and waves, covering electromagnetic and mechanical waves, optics and sound.
- Mechanics, including motion along a straight line, projectile motion, energy and power.
- Atomic, nuclear and thermal physics.
- Fields, e.g. force fields, gravitational fields, electrical fields, capacitors, electromagnetic induction, fundamental particles and particle accelerators.
- Quantum phenomena, including photo electricity, energy levels, photon emission and wave particle duality.
- Electricity: electrical quantities, resistance and resistivity, circuits and components, alternating current, direct current.
- Further mechanics, including momentum, circular motion and simple harmonic motion.

Courses can include practical applications of physics, which is also known as the Salters Horners approach to learning the subject.

Teaching is based on traditional lectures, discussions and practical work, e.g. learning experimental techniques, selecting and using different types of equipment, processing data, making measurements and observations and analysing results. Practical skills learned include using a wide range of apparatus, taking accurate readings and extracting information from a number of sources including graphs, practical data, textbooks and journals. Students must be prepared to do additional reading, e.g. from scientific journals, to fully understand the concepts covered.

Why study physics?

Physics makes significant contributions through advances in new technologies that arise from theoretical breakthroughs. For example, advances in the understanding of electromagnetism or nuclear physics led directly to the development of new products that have dramatically transformed modern-day society, such as television, computers, medical technology, domestic appliances and even nuclear weapons.

GCSE entry requirements

At least GCSE mathematics grade B/6, and grade B/6 in science and additional science are usually required.

How different from GCSE?

AS and A level are much more complex, with new topics not encountered at GCSE. Past students emphasise the need to work hard and not to be complacent if you get an A or A* at GCSE. There is a lot of mathematical content too.

How are the AS/A level assessed?

Assessment is broadly similar across the awarding bodies, with examinations comprising short answer, extended answer and multi-choice format questions, the proportions and exam timings being dependent on the awarding body used. Typically, AS level is assessed by two examination papers lasting 1½ hours each; A level is assessed by three examination papers ranging from 1½ to 2½ hours. A level includes a practical requirement (endorsement), meaning that students must pass at least 12 practical skills, although this does not contribute to the overall grade.

Combines well with

Mathematics and chemistry in particular, and to a lesser extent biology. Mathematics AS or A level is strongly recommended if you intend to take a degree in physics or any branch of engineering at university or aim to go into a higher or degree apprenticeship in engineering. Chemistry is recommended if you plan to take chemical engineering or materials engineering. Also combines well with design and technology or electronics for entry to university courses in product or engineering design.

Recent A level results

Total students: 32,419 **(Male: 25,472, Female: 6,947)** **Overall pass rate: 96.4%**

A*	A	B	C	D	E	U
8.9%	20.7%	22.4%	19.2%	15.1%	10.1%	3.6%

Higher education suitability

A facilitating subject, and so universally accepted for entry to any degree subject, as long as other requirements are met.

Case study

Dr Chris Handley took A levels in physics, mathematics and chemistry at Lady Hawkins School in Kington, Herefordshire. He said:

'Taking maths, physics and chemistry together creates a curriculum that enables much more practice of skills that are used in all three subjects, such as mathematics, algebra, statistics, critical thinking and some fundamental physics. The benefit of this for a student is that these skills are honed more quickly, and this reduces stress. Also, all these subjects by their nature require much less course work compared to humanities subjects, and more focus on practice. So having exercises that are transferable between all three subjects again speeds up that training.'

Physics at university

A level physics and mathematics are required to study physics at degree level in most cases; grade requirements can be high.

Physics degrees cover modern and classical physics, with the experimental techniques and mathematics that accompany them. Content will build on A level topics as above and will involve formal lectures, laboratory-based work and tutorials. There are 3-year BSc (Bachelor of Science) and 4-year MPhys (Master of Physics) or MSci (Master of Science) degrees; the latter are in fact undergraduate courses but go into greater depth than the BSc and give a good foundation for research and further study. Degree courses can offer specialist options such as astrophysics, applied physics, atmospheric physics and environmental physics, among others. Theoretical physics degrees involve a considerable amount of mathematics. There are sandwich degrees, most commonly on applied physics degrees, which involve an extended placement, usually 1 year, working in industry in the UK or abroad.

Physics can be combined with many other subjects at university, most commonly closely related subjects such as mathematics, electronics or astronomy. Aside from degrees, there are also Foundation degrees in physics, applied science and clinical technology where entry requirements are generally lower than for a degree.

Jobs with A level physics

There are higher and degree apprenticeships in engineering where A level physics and mathematics will usually be required. Below these there are advanced apprenticeships, which usually require GCSEs at grade C/5 or above in English language, mathematics and science or technology-based subjects. Higher and degree apprenticeships involve working for an employer and being funded by the government and employer to attend university or a college part time to take a Foundation degree, HNC/D (Higher National Certificate or Diploma) or degree qualification. There are also jobs and apprenticeships in laboratory work at technician level, e.g. in industry, schools and colleges. Outside of physics-based careers there are many other possibilities for employment where any A levels are acceptable, e.g. business administration, retail, customer service, management, banking and finance-based work including accounting. Search www.findapprenticeship.service.gov.uk/apprenticeshipsearch for vacancies.

Graduate level jobs in physics

Physics graduates can find employment in a wide range of industries, including the following.

- **Academic research:** e.g. in universities – physics graduates take higher degrees such as MSc and PhD in research and development in fields such as accelerator physics, astrophysics, plasma physics and radio imaging.
- **Engineering and electronics:** e.g. the research and development (R&D) of new products.
- **Medical physics:** the development of magnetic resonance imaging (MRI), ultrasound and scanning to diagnose disease and therapeutic radiography to treat cancers.
- **Space science.**
- **Teaching:** science teachers are in considerable demand.
- **The defence sector:** including the MOD (Ministry of Defence) and its contractors in the design and development of weapons, radar and satellite intelligence.
- **The energy industry:** e.g. gas, oil and electricity industries and also renewable sources such as wind, wave and solar power.
- **The materials industries:** including steel, plastics and ceramics producers.
- **The telecommunications industry.**
- **The transport industry.**

The computing sector employs many physics graduates and there are other occupational areas open to physics graduates, including business, finance, accountancy, local government and the civil service.

Further reading

Careers from physics: www.physics.org/careers

Institute of Physics (IOP): www.iop.org

Institute of Physics and Engineering in Medicine (IPEM): www.ipem.ac.uk

Psychology

Psychology is the scientific study of mind and behaviour. It will be of interest to students wanting to find out more about human thought and interaction. It is particularly useful for careers which involve significant contact with and working with people (see below for examples). A psychology degree is the most direct route to chartered (professional) psychologist status. Psychologists must not be confused with psychiatrists, who are in fact doctors of medicine who specialise in mental health. Do not study psychology with the expectation of conducting psychoanalysis or being trained to be a counsellor or therapist! Psychology is very much a science-based subject, particularly at degree level.

What do you study?

Precise course content depends on the awarding body syllabus followed, but areas covered can include the following.

- Key psychological concepts to explain behaviour: this includes theories and research based on different approaches in psychology, e.g. the biological approach (includes genetics and neurotransmitters), the behavioural approach (learning theory), the cognitive approach (is behaviour attributable to irrational thinking?), the psychodynamic approach (the unconscious mind) and the evolutionary approach (the idea of survival of the fittest and behaviour due to instinct).
- Research methods: how psychologists plan, design and conduct investigations, the collection and analysis of data, conducting statistical tests, the display of data using graphs and charts, forming scientific hypotheses and conclusions.

The subject is classroom based and includes discussions of different theories of why people think or behave as they do. There can be visits to conferences and universities, or meetings with famous psychologists and writers. As with other subjects, students must be prepared to read widely. Work experience in some form of helping/listening role can enhance a university application, e.g. helping young pupils with classroom learning and demonstrating what you learned from this experience. Also, a visit to talk with a professional psychologist will provide useful insight into the subject and its application. This is NOT part of the AS or A level course and would need to be arranged outside of teaching time.

Why study psychology?

The understanding of human behaviour is relevant to a wide range of careers, including those in human welfare, health, business, sport and artificial intelligence. The skills learned, e.g. analysing data and presenting well-structured written work, can be usefully applied to a wide range of careers.

GCSE entry requirements

GCSE mathematics at grade B/6 or above is often required, owing to statistical analysis that is covered, English language grade C/5 or above, and in some cases GCSE science grade C/5 or higher. Where GCSE psychology has been taken, a MINIMUM grade C/5 is likely to be required.

How different from GCSE?

Essays will be longer and need to demonstrate a greater depth of understanding than at GCSE. You will also probably need to make more contribution to class discussions. There is a lot of individual study, mostly reading around the subject to strengthen your knowledge. This is ESSENTIAL if higher grades are to be achieved. New topics will also be covered. Students comment on the large amount of information that needs to be learned and understood.

How are the AS/A level assessed?

AS and A level psychology are assessed by examinations only; there are no coursework components that contribute to the final grade. The format of examinations depends on the awarding body but can be a mix of compulsory and optional questions which are essay, multi-choice or short answer based. The awarding bodies in England all have two examination papers for AS level, each of 1½ hours' duration, and A level comprises three examinations, each of 2 hours' duration.

Combines well with

Biology especially, and mathematics is useful. Sociology and/or physical education are popular A level combinations with psychology. In fact psychology combines well with many subjects.

Recent A level results

Total students: 32,419 **(Male: 25,472, Female: 6,947)** **Overall pass rate: 96.4%**

A*	A	B	C	D	E	U
8.9%	20.7%	22.4%	19.2%	15.1%	10.1%	3.6%

Higher education suitability

Not a facilitating subject, but can be used for entry to a wide range of university courses, owing to the skills developed from the A level, e.g. essay writing, research, logical thinking and analysing data. Degrees such as economics, business, politics, sociology and geography and many others can all benefit from the skills acquired from A level psychology. In some instances psychology A level can count as a science.

Case study

Ellie Millerchip, from Heath Lane Academy Sixth Form in Leicestershire is taking psychology as one of her A level subjects. She said:

> *'I chose psychology as I wanted to learn about the working of the mind, which I find fascinating. I have learned things that I had never heard of and that you can relate to yourself and others around you. There is a LOT of work and some topics can be a bit confusing at times. There are more essays than I expected, so you need a good standard of English language to do this subject at A level. My future aim is a career in law and I have taken psychology as I felt that it would also give me a better understanding of why people behave as they do.'*

Psychology at university

A level psychology is not essential for entry to a degree, although it will demonstrate motivation to study it and will provide an insight into the subject. Universities vary in their requirements or preferences but science A levels, especially biology, will open up more university degree courses to applicants. I once heard an admissions tutor at a Russell Group university say that his 'ideal A level combination would be biology, mathematics and psychology', but he was by no means insistent on all of these. Psychology is a very popular degree subject, and for this reason alone, entry requirements can be high. ***A good grade in GCSE mathematics will often be required, grade B/6 or above.***

Students considering a career as a professional psychologist need to ensure that the degree is BPS (British Psychological Society) validated, as this is necessary for entry to postgraduate study and training for any of the branches of professional psychology. A non-BPS validated degree will require further study and examinations before Graduate Basis for Chartered Membership (GBC) is given.

A psychology degree can be a Bachelor of Arts (BA) or Bachelor of Science (BSc); this depends on the amount of quantitative analysis and experimental work covered. BA degrees are more oriented towards theories and topics that are less statistically based, e.g. they cover things such as theories of personality development and the ethics of psychology. However, ALL will cover statistical and quantitative analysis to some extent, so it is not a subject for the number-phobic! There are degrees that are more focused, e.g. health or sport psychology, and also those that are broader, such as cognitive science, which combines psychology with computer science, covering modelling of thought processes using computers (artificial intelligence), or behavioural science, which is often a combination of psychology and sociology, or biology, animal behaviour or anthropology. A psychology degree will typically cover areas such as development, perception, language learning, social relationships and abnormal psychology. Psychology can also be studied as a joint or combined degree with almost any other subject, although the more popular combinations include sociology, mathematics, computing, geography or management studies. Note the above BPS requirement if you intend seeking GBC. Joint or combined degrees may not have covered sufficient psychology content to be BPS validated, so always check with the universities and colleges offering such courses. Psychology can also be studied at Foundation degree and HND level; course titles include psychology, applied psychology, psychology and counselling, psychology and health studies, counselling and psychotherapy or animal behaviour and psychology.

Jobs with A level psychology

For non-graduates, jobs and apprenticeships tend to be health and care based in most instances, e.g. care assistant/social care assistant, and also in sport, e.g. fitness instructor or personal trainer. A level psychology is NOT a requirement for entry into these occupations. Psychology can be useful for a wide range of other types of work, e.g. business-based occupations such as marketing and human resources, as well as administrative and customer service type roles. A levels are not a general requirement for these sorts of work, although they can enhance prospects for getting into management-level roles later.

Graduate level jobs in psychology

A high degree classification (usually 2:1 honours) or above will usually be required to be able to go into postgraduate study, research and training leading to a master's degree or doctorate in one of the branches of psychology. These are the following.

- **Clinical psychology:** this covers working with patients in hospitals or within a community-based healthcare team.
- **Counselling psychology:** involves working with individuals, couples or families who are having difficulties with everyday life. May work privately, in GP surgeries, business or with counselling organisations. Some are self-employed.
- **Educational psychology:** this covers working with children with learning difficulties and/or behavioural problems and advising schools on strategies for the effective teaching and learning of such pupils. Usually employed by a local education authority.

- **Forensic psychology:** also known as legal or criminological psychology, covering assessment of the mental competence of offenders. They work with other professionals within the law court and prison systems.
- **Neurophysiology:** this involves working with people who have suffered brain injuries or trauma, such as a stroke, which has impaired their brain function. Rehabilitation is the focus of this branch of psychology. Work is mostly in the NHS or private medical sector.
- **Occupational psychology:** also known as industrial psychology, this covers the recruitment, training and development of staff using tools such as psychometric tests of aptitude and personality. Also covers improving the working environment, which can have a direct impact on performance at work.
- **Sport psychology:** this covers the link between the mind and sport performance. Sports psychologists work with individuals and teams in professional sport as well as recreational sport activity.

Only 20% of psychology graduates go on to become professional psychologists! [2]

Psychology is a valuable subject for entry into a wide range of occupations, especially those which involve a significant amount of human interaction, e.g. public relations, human resources, education, management, counselling, advertising, sales, marketing, social work, probation work, careers guidance and sport. It also has application to zoology (animal behaviour) and computing (artificial intelligence/human–computer interaction).

Further reading

The British Psychological Society: www.bps.org.uk

Careers in Psychology: www.careersinpsychology.co.uk

[2] Brian Heap, *HEAP 2018 – University Degree Course Offers 2018*, Trotman Education, p.480.

Religious studies

This subject is about the study of religious ethics, meaning the set of moral principles and values held by a religious group, and philosophy, the arguments used by religious groups to explain their beliefs. There is no need for students to be religious in any faith to benefit from studying it, and they are assessed on the merits of their arguments, not on their personal beliefs. Religious studies gives students a much better understanding of world religions, philosophy and ethics, and also of other people's views and how to see things from the perspectives of others. ***Religious studies AS/A level may challenge people's personal beliefs, which can be uncomfortable for some.***

What do you study?

Precise content will depend on the awarding body syllabus followed, but, broadly, courses will cover the following.

- Religious ethics: this looks at the relationship between religion and morality and the dilemmas that people can face. Coverage will include the theory of ethics, ethical language, objectivity, relativism, subjectivity, utilitarianism, law, justice and punishment, sexual ethics and war and peace. This aspect will draw on world religions for examples, and also modern media. Students will also look at the work of scholars such as Plato, Aristotle, Hume and Aquinas and their contributions to ethics and philosophy.
- Philosophy of religion: this looks at topics such as the philosophical arguments for the existence of God and the problems with these. It also covers study of the nature of God and the need to prove God's existence, the problem of evil, life after death, miracles and atheism.
- History of Christianity: this looks at the early Christian church as portrayed in the New Testament and its development through to medieval monasticism, the Reformation, non-conformity and Christianity in developing countries.
- Study of a particular world religion, e.g. Christianity, Hinduism, Islam, Judaism, Sikhism or Buddhism.
- Scriptures from particular religions.
- Religion and contemporary society.

Courses will involve study and research from books, television, videos, newspapers and journals, group discussions and debates, seminars (small group discussions with a tutor on a particular topic) and visits from speakers representing different ethical and philosophical positions.

Why study religious studies?

This subject will appeal to those who are interested in religion generally, and also to those who enjoy taking part in discussions and debates. The skills developed as outlined above are needed in a wide range of academic degree subjects at university, including law, politics, social sciences and language-based degrees, all of which require the ability to research information and present well-structured essays and arguments. These skills are valued by employers, as an ability to express oneself orally and/or in writing is required in many occupations.

GCSE entry requirements

GCSE grade C/5 or above in English language and/or history are often required, owing to the written demands of AS/A level religious studies.

How different from GCSE?

Some similarities of content, but topics will be studied in much more depth than those encountered at GCSE, and essays will need to be longer and show a higher level of understanding and analysis.

How are the AS/A level assessed?

For all awarding bodies, AS and A level are assessed by examinations only and these can involve structured answer and essay-format questions, in some cases divided into sections. Depending on the awarding body, the number of examination papers ranges from two to three for AS level and the same for A level. AS level exams range from 1 to 2 hours' duration. AQA has the longest examination papers for the A level, with two papers, each lasting 3 hours. Other boards mostly have three examination papers lasting 2 hours each for A level.

Combines well with

Religious studies can be combined with any other subjects, but particularly good combinations with it include classical subjects, archaeology, history, sociology, English literature, psychology and media studies. There is some overlap with sociology, classical civilisation and ancient languages.

Recent A level results

Total students: 27,032 **(Male: 8,215, Female: 18,817)** **Overall pass rate: 98.4%**

A*	A	B	C	D	E	U
5.2	18.3	31.1	25.8	13.4	4.6	1.6

Higher education suitability

Not a facilitating subject, but acceptable for entry to any degree subject, as long as other requirements are met. Religious studies can be used to enter other degree subjects such as law, American studies, history, politics, philosophy, social sciences, anthropology and teacher training or education studies.

Case study

James Roberts, from Hereford Cathedral School, took A level religious studies (RS) as one of his subjects. He said:

> *'I chose this subject because I enjoyed RS GCSE and I wanted to continue exploring the issues, ideas and concepts which I had begun to study. The topics covered at A level were similar to those at GCSE. However, at A level they were studied in greater detail. Furthermore, I was encouraged to engage with the ideas on a deeper level than I did at GCSE. Instead of simply articulating the idea of a philosopher, ethicist or theologian, I was encouraged to think independently and critically about their work. Also, as I was exposed to a greater range of ideas, there was more room at A level to write about my own interests. This A level stretched me to think for myself about very important issues. The course involves a lot of discussion, reading and writing which helped me to engage with arguments, to develop my own critical thinking, and to communicate in writing. Religious studies is a fascinating and extremely important subject to study. It is a broad discipline, and can cover philosophy, theology, biblical studies, ethics and more. I would encourage students to talk with prospective teachers about the course they run, to see how the course is shaped and how their individual interests may be reflected in the wide variety of material within this subject.'*

Religious studies at university

A level religious studies is not a general requirement for entry to a degree in the subject, although it will demonstrate interest and enhance a university application. At least one essay-based subject will usually be required.

There are many possibilities, including the study of major world religions, their history, moral issues they address and their place in contemporary society. A degree in divinity or theology will be based on Christianity; biblical studies deals with the Bible and its content plus the changing approaches to the Bible through the centuries. Some degree courses will focus on biblical Hebrew and/or Greek in the New Testament. There are also degrees in Jewish studies, Islamic studies and religion in the contemporary world, which explores the relationship between religion and society. Religious studies can be combined with many other subjects at university, the most popular including history, English, sociology, philosophy or languages. There are Foundation degree courses in Christian theology and ministry which are aimed at those intending to work in the Church. In addition, there are certificate and diploma courses which can be taken on a part-time basis, e.g. the University of Cambridge Certificate in Religious Studies, and which are taken by those planning a career in Christian ministry.

There are opportunities to study abroad as part of the degree or to study a particular religion over a holiday period. Course content can vary significantly, so it is very important to check the content of the degrees carefully and ensure that they will match your particular interests. Some degree courses offer flexibility in having the possibility to change option choices after the first year.

Jobs with A level religious studies

There are few, if any, jobs which would involve directly working in religion for people with this A level, but the skills learned from it are useful for a wide range of occupations requiring the ability to research information and express oneself clearly and effectively, whether orally or in writing. Content has relevance to working in areas such as health and social care, teaching assistant work and marketing, where an awareness of and sensitivity to different cultures and religions can be needed.

Graduate level jobs in religious studies

These include:

- museum curatorship
- professional roles in a particular religion, e.g. Church ministry in the Christian faith.
- teaching
- university lecturing and research.

Aside from the above, there are also many other possibilities for religious studies graduates. Some go into caring/welfare-based professions, others into charitable work, and there are many other areas where employers will accept any degree subject for entry, including business administration, accountancy, banking and finance, management, customer service, retail management or journalism (postgraduate study and training will be required for the latter).

Further reading

RE:ONLINE: www.reonline.org.uk

Sociology

Sociology is part of a group of subjects called 'social sciences'. The social sciences also include anthropology, economics, politics and social psychology. These use scientific methods to try to describe and understand how we live and work together.

Sociology is closely related to psychology, but while psychology focuses on individuals, sociology looks at people in groups. A group could be as large as the population of the UK, or as small as a family.

Sociologists are interested in the customs, traditions and social institutions that exist in different societies. Examples of social institutions are: marriage, work, the family, schools, government, social class, the legal system.

Sociologists use scientific methods to investigate social groups. Their methods include the following.

- Document studies: using statistics and other published information.
- Experiments: e.g. observing people's behaviour in carefully controlled conditions to establish cause-and-effect relationships.
- Participant observation: where the sociologist becomes involved in the lives of the people concerned, e.g. by joining a club or gang.
- Surveys: collecting information from people by questionnaires and/or interviews.

Sociology experiments can be difficult to perform because of the variety of different elements (e.g. different upbringings and beliefs) involved when looking at humans in groups.

What do you study?

Precise content will depend on the awarding syllabus followed. Typically, content will include the following.

- Research methods: how sociologists obtain information and the advantages and disadvantages of the methods used.
- Education: the link between social class, social mobility and education, achievement and gender, educational institutions.
- The family: the different types of family structures, the position of children in families and wider society, marriage, divorce, gender roles.
- Religion in society.
- Welfare, poverty and health: what is poverty? Why does it persist? The role of the welfare state.

- Deviance: what is antisocial behaviour? What causes crime? The role of the media in defining deviance. How social order is achieved through laws and accepted codes of behaviour.
- Politics and power: political parties, ideologies, pressure groups, feminism and environmentalism, political institutions.
- Communities and nations: how these are formed and maintained, relationships between nations.
- The sociology of youth: youth culture and subcultures, the role of the media in popular culture, young people and education.
- Global sociology: development/underdevelopment, industrialisation and the environment, political, cultural and economic relationships between societies.

AS and A level sociology are classroom based but can include discussions, use of DVDs, the internet and newspaper articles to illustrate how the subject relates to the world. Visits to places such as law courts, and visits from guest speakers representing particular services or religions can also take place. Sociology is an essay-based subject and will require a LOT of reading, which is crucial if a high grade is to be achieved.

Why study sociology?

It is a useful and relevant subject to occupational areas such as social work, probation work, careers guidance, the prison service, the police, counselling, market research, care management and human resources.

Skills developed include: communication, analysis and report writing, which are transferable to a wide range of careers.

GCSE entry requirements

GCSE English language and mathematics at grade 4/5 or above will usually be required. GCSE sociology is not a requirement, but if it has been taken a grade C/5 or above will likely be expected.

How different from GCSE?

Not a widely available subject at GCSE, but AS and A level rely on your ability to use information sources a lot more. Essays will be longer and need to demonstrate a greater depth of understanding and analysis. You will also probably need to make more contribution to class discussions, especially where group sizes are smaller. Much wider reading will be required than at GCSE.

How are the AS/A level assessed?

AQA and OCR AS level are assessed by two examination papers, each lasting 1½ hours. AQA A level is assessed by three examinations, each lasting 2 hours. OCR also has three examination papers for A level but one paper lasts 1½ hours and two papers last 2¼ hours. Question format depends on the awarding body and can be short answer or essay based, with compulsory and/or optional questions.

Combines well with

Psychology, government and politics, economics, geography. As some sociology degrees (BSc, Bachelor of Science) can involve quantitative analysis, a number-based subject such as mathematics or statistics at AS or A level is recommended if you are intending to take a BSc degree.

Recent A level results

Total students: 33,980 **(Male: 7,848, Female: 26,132)** **Overall pass rate: 97.9%**

A*	A	B	C	D	E	U
5.6	13.2	27.1	28.7	16.9	6.4	2.1

Higher education suitability

Not a facilitating subject, but accepted for entry to a wide range of university subjects, including social sciences, business, management and marketing, as long as other requirements are met.

Case study

Katie Steptoe, a sixth form student at Heath Lane Academy in Leicestershire, is taking A levels in sociology, psychology and health and social care, with the aim of training to be a paramedic at university. Regarding sociology, she said:

> *'I chose sociology as I thought it would link well with my other subjects. It was completely new to me and at first the essays seemed scary but they are OK once you get into the way of writing A level-standard essays, which are longer and more analytical than those we wrote at GCSE. Sociology gives a better understanding of different cultures and issues that anyone in a helping or caring career needs to know. It is a very interesting subject and I would definitely recommend it to others.'*

Sociology at university

A level sociology is not generally necessary to study the subject at university, although taking it will demonstrate interest and motivation. Humanities such as history or geography are useful. It would be wise to include an essay-based subject in A level choices, given that sociology is very much an essay/extended response type of subject at university.

Sociology can be taken as a BA (Bachelor of Arts) or BSc. In the latter case it will have a scientific/quantitative approach, so check the content of degree courses carefully. The first year of sociology degree courses often gives a general introduction to social sciences, e.g. social policy, economics, psychology or politics. degree courses in year one can cover topics covered at A level, with second and third-year topics being more specialised, e.g. gender and sexuality, religion, race, social justice or social policy. Sociology can also been combined with many other subjects at university, with the more common including psychology, politics, economics, history, applied sociology or social work. In the latter two cases, these degrees will include assessed work-based practice, which can lead towards qualifying as a social worker.

There are Foundation Degrees in subjects where sociology is a significant component, e.g. public services, housing, youth and community development, health and housing. There are also HNC/D courses in subjects such as social care management, social studies or social sciences. Entry requirements for Foundation degree and HNC/D (Higher National Certificate or Diploma) courses are generally lower than for a degree.

Jobs with A level sociology

Sociology is very useful for the police service, prison service, care work and a range of business-based roles, including marketing and human resources. A levels are not a general requirement to apply for jobs and apprenticeships in these sorts of occupation, although having them will enhance future possibilities such as progression into management roles.

Graduate level jobs in sociology

Examples of occupations that involve working in sociology where a degree (not necessarily in sociology) is usually required are:

- counselling
- probation work
- professional sociologist/university lecturer
- social work
- sociology teaching in schools and colleges.

There are also jobs in the health and care sector, e.g. care assistant with children or the elderly. These do not require a degree or indeed any particular academic qualifications, unless specified by the employer.

Further reading

British Sociological Association (BSA): www.britsoc.co.uk

Appendix 1
The awarding bodies

AQA (Assessment and Qualifications Alliance)
www.aqa.org.uk

CCEA (Council for the Curriculum, Examinations and Assessment) – Northern Ireland examination board
https://ccea.org.uk

OCR (Oxford, Cambridge and Royal Society of Arts)
www.ocr.org.uk

Pearson Edexcel – awarding body for A level and BTEC qualifications
https://qualifications.pearson.com

WJEC (Welsh Joint Education Committee) Eduqas
www.wjec.co.uk

Appendix 2 Some useful information sources

There are many careers sites and books available – the following are examples.

Careers and general information websites

National Careers Service – includes job profiles of many occupations, including the qualification requirements for them.
https://nationalcareersservice.direct.gov.uk

Not Going to Uni – compares apprenticeships, gap years, jobs and distance learning as alternatives to going to university full time.
www.notgoingtouni.co.uk

Prospects – contains information on a wide range of topics, including jobs for graduates in particular university subjects.
www.prospects.ac.uk

Push – includes information on the reasons for choosing to go to university, as well as details about UK universities and taking a gap year.
www.push.co.uk

Studential – has information on further education (including A levels), taking a gap year, higher education, apprenticeships and British Army options.
www.studential.com

There are also many licensed careers software packages; check with the sixth form or college you go to on availability.

Higher education information

Student finance (www.gov.uk) – this website includes a student finance calculator which gives an estimate of the money you would get to go to university. You apply for university finance through this site.
www.gov.uk/student-finance

HE Map – shows the locations of UK universities and other higher education institutions.
www.scit.wlv.ac.uk/ukinfo

The Student Room – contains all sorts of information for students, including useful advice on studying A levels effectively.
www.thestudentroom.co.uk

UCAS – has extensive information on applying to university and also a search facility for higher education courses which links directly to university sites.
www.ucas.com

Unistats – the official site for comparing UK universities, including course data, student satisfaction, jobs and salaries after graduation.
http://unistats.ac.uk

HEAP 2018: University Degree Course Offers by Brian Heap (Trotman Education) – a yearly publication which gives details of university entrance requirements for particular subjects, including GCSE, A level grades/UCAS Tariff points, which universities interview, examples of questions that can arise at interviews and why students are rejected.

The Times Good University Guide by John O'Leary (Times Books) – a yearly publication which provides league tables of universities by subject, based on levels of student satisfaction, employability, teaching quality and research.

Appendix 3
Alternatives to A levels

There are other qualifications that can be taken instead of or combined with A levels. The alternatives available will depend on provision in your area. Subjects/ courses can be found by using the course search facility on www.ucasprogress.com. Below are the most commonly available Level 3 qualifications.

BTECs

These are vocational qualifications that introduce students to broad occupational sectors, e.g. business or engineering, although some subjects are more specialist. They are more practical than A levels and students complete assignments and projects based on real workplace situations, and some subjects include work experience. For entry into BTECs generally a minimum of 4 or 5 GCSEs at grade C/4 or 5 are required, often to include one or more from English language, mathematics and science. See https://qualifications.pearson.com.

International Baccalaureate (IB)

The IB Diploma usually takes 2 years to complete and covers a broader range of subjects than A levels. Six subjects are studied, including mathematics, your own language, a foreign language, a humanities subject, a science and an arts subject. It is taught in schools in over 140 countries and is a well-recognised entry qualification to university, owing to both the depth and breadth of study it involves. See www.ibo.org.

Cambridge Technicals

Cambridge Technicals are vocational qualifications in which students specialise in specific subject areas: art and design, business, health and social care, ICT, leisure and recreation, media and communication, performing arts and science and sport. GCSE subject and grade requirements for Level 3 courses are broadly the same as for entry to BTECs at Level 3. See www.cie.org.uk.

Cambridge Pre-U

The Cambridge Pre-U Diploma comprises a number of principal subjects, plus what are known as the core Global Perspectives and Research element (GPR). Students have a free choice of three principal subjects from a menu of 27. See www.cie.org.uk.

AQA Baccalaureate

This is studied in Years 12 and 13 and includes three A levels and either an AS level or a fourth A level as well as mandatory enrichment activities and an extended project (Extended Project Qualification – EPQ).

GCSE requirements are broadly the same as for A level entry. See www.aqa.org.uk/programmes/aqa-baccalaureate.

Welsh Baccalaureate (Welsh Bacc)

This is available in schools and colleges in Wales and comprises two parts:

- **core**, consisting of essential skills, Wales, Europe and the World (includes a language option), work-related education, personal and social education and an individual investigation
- **options**, consisting of principal learning and a project with other options which can be AS/A levels, GCSEs or BTECs, depending on the level of Welsh Bacc qualification.

See www.welshbaccalaureate.org.uk for further information.

Scottish Baccalaureate

Four subject areas are available: expressive arts, sciences, social sciences and languages. The Baccalaureate comprises Scottish Higher and Advanced Higher qualifications plus an interdisciplinary project that enables candidates to develop and show evidence of initiative, responsibility and independent working, which are valuable for entry into higher education and employment. See www.sqa.org.uk/baccalaureates for details.

Access to HE (Higher Education) Diploma or Access course

The Access Diploma is for students age 19+ who do not hold the qualifications required for university entry. It can usually be completed in 1 year full time or 2 years part time. Some courses are linked to specific universities and/or subjects.

Occupational qualifications: apprenticeships (jobs with training)

Training can be done in the traditional 'day release' way by going to a college one day per week or can include block release, where trainees attend college or training full time for a set period. Apprentices work towards a main occupational qualification, such as an NVQ (National Vocational Qualification), and technical certificates that build the knowledge base required by the work they are doing.

How to decide on A levels or alternatives

It is important to base your decision on which qualification pathway you take (A level or alternative) on the following factors.

- How you learn best: are you better in more theory-based subjects and able to tackle exams well? Are you more of a practical/applied learner who prefers a more project/assignment-based approach, including working with others?
- What type of qualification is required for the university course or occupation(s) you are considering? For example, the A level, AQA Bacc or IB routes would be needed for entry to medicine, veterinary science or dentistry.
- What is available in your area?

Appendix 4
Higher education qualifications

Higher education and qualifications mean education and qualifications that are above A level standard. They are most commonly taken at universities but are also available at some colleges of higher education or by distance learning, e.g. at the Open University. The most commonly available qualifications are the following.

Degree

Also known as a 'bachelor's', 'first' or 'undergraduate' degree, the most common are the BA (Bachelor of Arts) and BSc (Bachelor of Science). Others include BEd (Bachelor of Education), BMus (Bachelor of Music), BEng (Bachelor of Engineering) and LLB (Bachelor of Law), but there are more. Bachelor's degrees usually take three years to complete, and four if you are taking a 'sandwich' degree, which includes an extended placement working in the industry/sector that you are studying. Some degrees take longer, e.g. medicine or dentistry which are 5-year courses followed by further training.

Foundation degree

This qualification is most commonly FdA (Foundation degree in Arts) or FdSc (Foundation degree in Science) and is usually completed in two years, or three if a sandwich option is offered. Students follow a mix of academic study and work-based learning linked to particular types of occupation. Entry requirements are generally lower than for a degree. There is often the option of 'topping up' the Foundation degree to a bachelor's degree with further study (usually one or two years).

Higher National Certificate (HNC) or Diploma (HND)

These are work-related qualifications covering a wide range of occupational areas. HNDs take two years to complete full time, or three years for sandwich courses. HNC is essentially the part time version of the HND, often taken by people in occupations connected to the qualification e.g. engineering or business. HNCs can be taken full time in 1 year, with a further year to top up to HND, and 1 or 2 more years to gain a bachelor's degree. Entry requirements are broadly the same as for Foundation degrees.

Diploma of Higher Education

DipHE is the first 2 years of a degree, giving students the option of completing their studies in 2 years and achieving a higher education qualification. Academically it is considered equivalent to HND, and likewise it can be topped up to a degree with further study (usually 1 year).

Certificate of Higher Education (CertHE)

CertHE is equivalent to the first year of a full honours degree. It is the most basic level of qualification that can be gained in higher education and shows that you are capable of studying successfully at university level. You can use a CertHE as the first step to one of the above qualifications.

Diploma in Foundation Studies

This is a one-year course, covering a range of subjects in the general area of art and design, including fine art, graphic and 2D design, photography, fashion and textiles. It enables students to build a strong portfolio of work and is often a requirement for entry to higher education courses in creative design subjects. AS/A level art and design are not always required to enter a course, as long as proof of artistic ability can be shown e.g. through a portfolio. ***Do not confuse the Diploma in Foundation Studies with a Foundation degree!***

How to decide on higher education qualifications

Which of the above undergraduate courses you take will depend on:

- what career/university subject you want to pursue
- the A level grades you are likely to achieve.

For certain careers, e.g. law or psychology, it is important that the course you take is recognised by the relevant professional bodies, and in many cases a DEGREE will be required for entry. Table 3 (pages 12–16) lists the requirements for entry to the more popular university subjects.

Appendix 5
Qualifications: a classification

At the time of writing, the qualifications in the following table were correct. The table gives a general guide to how qualifications compare with each other. However, universities and employers will have their own preferences as to the TYPE of qualifications they accept. BTECs are given here as examples of vocational qualifications, but qualifications are also available from other awarding bodies, some of which are linked to specific occupational areas. These will be stated in particular institutions' prospectuses/sites. ***Compiled using the Regulated Qualifications Framework.***

Qualification level	Work based	Vocational	Academic	Employment level
Levels 7–8	Professional diplomas	Postgraduate diplomas and certificates	Doctorates and master's degrees	Professional and senior management
Levels 4–6	NVQ Levels 4 and 5	Foundation degrees (level 5), HNDs (level 5), HNCs (level 4)	Honours degrees (level 6)	Management/ supervisory
Level 3	NVQ Level 3 and other job-specific qualifications at level 3	BTEC Level 3 qualifications	A levels, AS levels, International Baccalaureate, Cambridge Pre U	Technician
Level 2	NVQ Level 2 and other job specific qualifications at level 2	BTEC First/Level 2 Diploma	GCSEs grade A*–C/new grades 9–4 Functional Skills Level 2 (English, Maths, ICT)	Skilled
Level 1	NVQ Level 1 and other job-specific qualifications at level 1	BTEC Introductory Diploma Level 1	GCSEs grade D–G/new grades 3–1 Functional Skills Level 1 (English, Maths, ICT)	Semi-skilled
Entry Level	Foundation Learning	Foundation Learning	Foundation Learning Functional Skills Entry Levels 1, 2, 3 (English, Maths, ICT)	Unskilled